REFLECTIONS ON THAT OTHER AMERICA

by

Ivan H. Nothdurft

International Standard Book Number
ISBN 0-934426-66-X

Library of Congress Catalog Card Number
LCCN 95-95357

Available from:

IHN Publications
733 N. Sunset Blvd.
Cape Girardeau, MO 63701

Manufactured in the U.S.A.
by

Stewart Printing & Publishing Co.
Route 1, Box 646
Marble Hill, MO 63764
Toll Free (800) 758-8629

To

LORLA, my wife, and co-worker,
who has helped with the organization,
revision, and typing of the manuscript.

TABLE OF CONTENTS

CONTENTS cont'd

FOREWORD

That other America consists of a dozen self-hoods or nations—countries which are far different than the states of the United States. Each country has its own distinct characteristics, attitudes, and approaches to situations. The basic or fundamental needs of life for food, shelter, and general well-being are much the same—although met and served in somewhat different ways.

Each glimpse herein is meant to show similarities or contrasts in the cultures of the Americas and is not intended to imply that what may be true in one is also true in all. Above all these reflections are meant to show respect for the people of those lands.

Ivan H. Nothdurft
Cape Girardeau, Missouri
January 1996

A DIFFERENT APPROACH

Why does Fidel Castro rant and rave for hours with an audience seemingly listening attentively? One sometimes wonders why people in other countries do not act in the way one would expect. Custom in Latin America seems to demand that one never say in a few words what one can say in a page or more. Whereas we say we prefer a speaker who can compact a profound message in a few words like a Gettysburg address, the people of that other America usually prefer a lengthy oration with all the color and flowery language that the speaker can muster. They consider it a matter of skill and artistry. They are impressed by the orator who can "turn a phrase and paint a word picture," regardless of the time required. Then he will possibly close his lengthy oration with the ex cathedra ending "He dicho" (I have spoken) as if to say, "Thus saith the Lord."

In the United States a person who has a difference of opinion with another person might ask for a moment to speak with that person in private to tell him of his thoughts. I have noticed that the Latins tend to express their thoughts publicly to the other person in no uncertain terms. Once while attending a meeting in Rio de Janeiro, Brazil a delegate asked for the floor and then told another member of the group what a terrible person he was. He really opened up and let him have it. The person who had been attacked asked to speak and responded just as loudly and vociferously to his attacker. The first speaker, realizing that he had possibly gone too far, spoke again softening his attack and criticism of the other. The second person then responded with an equal softening. After a few such exchanges, with gradual softening on each side it wasn't long before each was complimenting the other. Then they came to the front of the room and gave each other an "abrazo" (embrace). At that moment the chair of the Bible Society meeting arose and said, "Gentlemen, I think it is time for a word of prayer, a breath of air, and a cup of coffee." The matter was settled.

At a meeting of Spanish speaking pastors in New York City, a gentleman was greatly annoyed by something that was said which he thought very degrading to him. He said he was deeply hurt by that attack, that he was resigning and would not attend those meetings again and stormed out of the room. At the next meeting I was almost amazed to see the offended person among the first to appear. He apologized to the group and expressed his appreciation for the members and said that he planned to continue his support and cooperation.

As director of the Escuela America (American School) in La Victoria, Lima, Peru, I would frequently receive a note from a parent asking that I excuse Juancito from school that day as "Él está de purgante." (He has taken a purgative.) That is not a common excuse in the U.S. but would probably be just as effective. There seemed to be a tendency to speak frankly.

A less direct approach was the "messenger" sent to ask for another's interest. When the boarding student wanted to get permission, or to request the purchase of some personal item, he or she would send another student to make the request, or in some cases, the "messenger" would accompany the student, but the messenger would be the one to voice the request. Everyone does that occasionally but to us it seemed that the students would use this method much more frequently than was required in other settings.

A friend, Bob Schlager, in Buenos Aires, Argentina, complained about the fact that when his house was built, he had planned an opening for a pipe to carry all the wires which would be needed so he could have the telephone or any other kind of cable or wire inserted therein. The workers were not used to that kind of pre-planning and the wall was closed. When the men arrived to make the installation for the electricity, no pipe could be found. They had to chip out a hole through the wall, then make the installation, and close or patch up the hole. Then the telephone men arrived and again chipped a hole and patched it. The process was repeated yet another time for the TV. It was not uncommon to pour the floor and then chip out a path for whatever pipes were needed.

As a pastor in Lima, Peru in the 1940s, I occasionally called on a family. The woman had two sons, both in their twenties, both employed, but still living at home. I noticed that there was a big hole in the middle of the living room floor. I kept wondering when one of the young men would do something so their mother wouldn't have to risk walking into the hole each time she went through the room. Weeks and months passed but no one did anything to repair or cover the hole. The young men claimed they were too busy at their jobs to do anything and the mother was poor and didn't have funds to have it done. It was probably a question of priority. After all these years I wonder if anything was ever done to that hole in the middle of the living room floor.

Have you ever prepared to shake someone's hand in greeting only to discover that no one responded? In that other America one not only shakes hands but must be prepared for an embrace. There seems to be an art in knowing just how to embrace the other person, and one may feel a bit awkward at first, but one soon gets used to the custom. Some Argentinians like to tell the story of two Chileans who met after not having seen each other for quite a while. They shook hands and then had a long embrace. Then they shook hands again, and each left with the other's wallet.

Although the "abrazo" was a customary way of greeting, it seemed to radiate a genuine interest and concern for the well being of the other person and unrestrained delight at their meeting. There was always time for a short chat. There was a graciousness and charm which often is lacking in our fast-paced busy world.

5

FIRST IMPRESSIONS OR THE TRUTH?

At one time I was amused at the disregard for truth and accuracy in that other America. I would become lost en route to some place and I would ask for directions. I would be given an elaborate and detailed description as to how to get to where I wanted to go. In time, I would learn that the person had no idea of the desired destination, but to hide his ignorance, he would direct me on my way while joyfully wishing me a safe and pleasant journey. Sooner or later I would be chagrined at his blatant deception. The general attitude was to say what would please one at the moment. Truth was secondary. What he wanted to do was to impress me with his knowledge and to please or make me feel good.

Despite our differences, there is still that basic or underlying desire to make a good impression. There is a lot of deception in the world, and although our methods may differ, the overwhelming desire to please or impress and to look better than we think we are is rather fundamental. Before the extreme emphasis on cosmetic and plastic surgery or breast implantation, one can remember the promotion of falsies and other such means to give that best though possibly inaccurate impression.

It seems rational for one to "put one's best foot forward." It was that first impression which counted. In my work as pastor in Peru, I would see people looking like a million dollars who had often spent a disproportionate amount of their income to dress lavishly in order to gain attention or to impress others. They were often so well dressed and cosmetically perfect that one would get a wrong impression. Everyone wears a mask or disguise to a greater or lesser degree. I wondered at first why people would give me an incorrect address or information as to where they lived. I would later discover that they lived in a hovel, and that at times was embarrassing to both of us.

This tendency to disguise ourselves was apparent also in the arrangement and appearance of homes. The facade must be beautiful. The "sala" must be attractive and pleasant while the rear or back of the place could be unkempt and often desolate. Even churches sometimes presented the same picture, a beautiful and expensive exterior and facade, but the back was quite run down and unattractive.

Of course, I have also seen young people in the U.S. out cruising in the finest automobiles imaginable. I have wondered if the vehicle was a gift, or possibly rented to impress one with their wealth and life style.

I have been the guest of people in that other America who have invited me to a lunch or dinner at an exclusive restaurant, and who have ordered only the finest to impress me. A friend invited six or eight of us to dine with him. Later I discovered that he had gone far beyond his means. It is often typical for a Latin to be "theatrically" generous in order to give a good impression, although a mistaken one.

My first impression of students in Bolivia and Peru in the late 1940s was quite the same. Cheating on exams was common, and to challenge it was a waste of time. I recall asking a fellow professor in our mission school in Cochabamba, Bolivia to help proctor an exam. He did and then I discovered he was going down the aisles helping students to get the answer required. I noticed that he was especially attentive to the prettier young ladies. The general idea was that cheating was O.K. The sin was in getting caught.

This same attitude has become increasingly apparent in the U.S I have just heard a discussion on the disregard for truth and accuracy on the part of the media. Our press at times tends to print anything without fully verifying the validity of the reporting. The press will even report news from the tabloids occasionally without checking for accuracy. The criteria is to print what the public wants to read, that which will sell or make money for the producer. The so called "yellow journalism"' is now something which one reads about in history books.

Talk show hosts may say what they please without always verifying the actual facts, usually walking that thin line which will avoid litigation. Otherwise, who cares if it is true or not? If it is interesting and titillating enough to get an audience and to make money, it doesn't have to be valid. I think that our friends from down under in South America have been a whole step ahead of us in this area of integrity. Recent revelations of serious deviations from the moral code or system in U.S Military academies suggest that we, too, may be catching on.

9

ADAPTABLE?

Four Railway express men in Missouri had struggled to hoist a large wooden box of our belongings onto a truck to start the shipment to Bolivia. Then, on arrival in Cochabamba, Bolivia, a diminutive Indian fellow, chewing his coca (cocaine) leaves, placed a rope around the box, lifted the box onto his back and shoulder and carried that box into the house alone. Evidently the coca was enough to adjust his strength. He had adapted, and there I was watching , just trying to inhale enough oxygen of that rarified air to keep mobile. Cochabamba was at an altitude of 8,500 feet.

There were other signs of the adaptability of those indigenous people. Many seldom, if ever, wore shoes, but after years of going barefoot their feet seemed to be so tough and calloused that it seemed they were wearing some kind of sandal. This caused me to remember how the Incas had used runners to carry messages over that rocky terrain from town to town, a kind of early forerunner of the pony express in our country. That adaptability was even more evident when I sat in a compartment while on a train trip between La Paz, Bolivia and Antofagasta, Chile. Looking out the window I saw dozens of children running around and playing on the ice and snow covered ground. They were running in their bare feet, and obviously warm while I was fully clad and shivering from the cold. They had adapted so well that they were oblivious to the climate

In 1945 the McGraw Warren Construction Company was building a section of the Pan American Road system, which was to run through Santa Cruz and on to Corumbá on the Brazilian border. Mr. Al Hosking, who was somewhat of a humanitarian, decided to do something for the workers who were mainly Indians. He had bunkhouses built with the added convenience of showers with hot and cold running water. Some said that the "Indios" would never use them. However, they did and seemed to enjoy those hot showers for more than the usual amount of time. Small hospital shacks were also built to care for the sick or injured. Once the laborers were put in beds between sheets (instead of sleeping on the ground) and had meals brought to them, they did not want to leave. It was said that the "Indios" would even injure themselves just for the luxury of that special care but this was never proven. It did show that adaptability was a two way street. A person could adapt upward as well as downward.

The U.S. Point Four program in Bolivia and Peru in the 1940s made some excellent contributions. The area had been known as the original home of the Irish potato of which there were hundreds of varieties. The Indian cultivated them on the side of the mountain where he was obliged to have a small garden piece of ground and harvested small marble sized potatoes. At first he was a bit suspicious of the larger "papas" but he readily adapted to the use of the larger potato and soon his "papas a la Huancaina" were as big and delectable as could be found anywhere.

I noticed that there were marked class distinctions in Bolivia and Peru. Their apparel helped to identify them. There were the “Indios" (Indians), the "Cholos" or half breeds (“mestizos”), and then there were the "gente" or people, who usually wore European type clothing. The "gente", of course, were the predominant force in the power structure. The "Indios" and "Cholos" had pretty much adapted to their place in society.

I would take Saturnino, our gardener, along to the "cancha" or market to buy potatoes or other staples which he would carry back for me. I could not convince him to walk beside me. He would trot along a couple of steps behind me like a little puppy. He would always reply, "Señor, tu eres el patrón, y no puedo caminar a tu lado." (You are the master. I can not walk beside you). Saturnino said he was going to get married. I had previously met some of his children and grandchildren. Then I learned the reason for his contemplated step. He owned a small garden sized plot of ground, and he was trying to be sure that his heirs would be able to inherit it. He was adapting to the laws of the country.

He had long enjoyed and also suffered from too much "chicha" (corn alcohol which I think was once called "white mule” here in our part of Missouri.) It was claimed that "Chicha Cliseña" was by far the best because the sexiest women from that pueblo would chew the corn and spit it into the vat to begin the fermentation process. These beautiful women were said to produce the highest quality of “chicha.” I thought it appropriate that anyone who sold "chicha" would hang a small white flag in front of his place to let the world know that he had chicha for sale. To me it meant "surrender" and to a degree that was what it meant to many. That adaptation was too much for some.

One day we found old Saturnino fallen between the plants and flowers which he so much adored and cared for. He was not simply under a "chicha" binge but had expired. He had adapted to a simple life with no complaints.

Then there was Crispín. He was supposedly a "jack of all trades" or handy man. He was younger and much stronger than Saturnino, so he could work harder. He seemed to have rather shifty eyes and a cunning look that made it difficult for me to trust him. He knew we were not going to overlook shoddy work. He responded to our demands and became a very loyal worker. I guess he adapted to us as much as we did to him. The adaptability was so mutual that we really appreciated his work, and he adapted to our demands for neatness and punctuality, a rare commodity .

Victoria was a somewhat overweight kitchen and cleaning maid in the school in Cochabamba. She did everything, even more than we knew. One morning she had carried some heavy bags of staples from the warehouse to the kitchen. Later on, Victoria was nowhere to be found. We were told that she had gone to the hospital to have her baby. We were rather dumbfounded since we didn't even know that she was expecting. The Indian women there wear several full skirts one over the other. They are said to remove the outer skirt once each year on their birthday and add another clean one underneath. I never bothered to check this out. She returned carrying little Carlitos who was soon the pride and joy of the whole staff. Victoria's sister could not bear children and her husband had been the sire. This was another case of adaptability.

The women also wore distinctive hats which noted the village or town in which they lived. In our city they wore large white stovepipe hats which they repainted each year and which got heavier as time went by. It seemed strange that women should agree to wear the same style of hat just because they lived in a certain town. In our culture that would take quite a bit of adjustment.

The "Indios" were not a sedentary lot. They seemed to be almost always on the move. They would walk along with a small child on their back, tending a flock of llamas, and spinning a spindle of yarn at their sides. They had adapted to the necessities of life.

And who could forget the pets. There were two or three dogs, a goat, and some ducks who belonged, I believe, to the laundress. Those animals had adapted to each other and seemed to enjoy marching around together all around the place. They would walk into the open door of classrooms unannounced and apparently unnoticed. The school children had adapted so well to the scenario that they didn't seem to notice the intrusion of the animal parade each time they marched duck fashion through a class room. I knew that I was less adaptable than were those students.

At that time in 1945 the elementary section of our mission school, Colegio Americano in Cochabamba was quartered in an old tapia (packed earth) two-story house. The walls were about four feet wide. Typical of the houses of that time the rooms were built around a patio. In addition to the school rooms, part of the building was used as a dormitory for thirteen girls in the boarding department, four teachers, and our three-room apartment. However there was only one complete bathroom plus one other toilet and I was the only male!

There was also a large "loro" or parrot who loved to perch on a wire on the back balcony. One of the teachers complained that the loro had eaten all the polka dots off her dress which had been hanging there. Few noticed him or he them, but he and I didn't like each other. We didn't adapt at all. One day he perched on the electric wire. He seemed to like the insulation and was soon electrocuted. That was one less adjustment for me to make. No longer would he squawk at me or threaten me, and I didn't grieve that much over his demise.

I left Bolivia after a year because I couldn't adapt or adjust to the altitude although the climate was quite agreeable and the geraniums grew as tall as the second story. I became tense and short of breath. The doctors said that I would do better at sea level. I could not adapt to the altitude. I'll never forget those "indios" and their remarkable ability to adapt to difficult and confusing situations.

Now fifty years later, I am sure that even under changing conditions these remarkable people still have the ability to adapt to the world about them.

"¿QUÉ ME IMPORTA LA LEY?"

When our personal belongings finally arrived via ship and rail to Cochabamba, Bolivia, it became a wonderful experience. Our belongings seemed like long lost friends. It was good to see them again. Then came that most confusing task of getting them through "aduana" or customs. We hired an agent, reportedly honest, and agreed to pay the stipulated fee. Everything was proceeding nicely until one of the workers dropped my typewriter to the floor and smashed it. He was careless, and I suppose my retort was about the same. I claimed that he would have to pay since the law (ley) would hold him responsible. He smiled and answered, "¿Qué me importa la ley?" (The law means nothing to me.) I learned that he was right. All I got was my broken typewriter.

I learned that there are many ways to get around the law. A common saying is "Hecha la ley; hecha la trampa" which loosely translated meant "Pass a law; find the loophole." Murray and Nova Dickson and Lorla and I were to travel to La Paz on a Sunday morning train. We had secured our certificate of good health which was required to travel from one town to another. But Saturday evening we realized we had not gotten the identification certificate. Murray, who had been there longer than I, volunteered to get them that evening. He returned a while later and had the four permits. They even included the "impresiones digitales" (finger prints). I asked how he had done it. He said that the law required finger prints, he had used his thumb for his and the other thumb for mine, and had done the same with fingers for the I.D. of our wives. With this adaptation or interpretation of the law, the four of us traveled to La Paz without incident or question.

One day Murray and I were talking in the garden when I suddenly saw a fellow running down the sidewalk carrying a bicycle on his shoulders. I said to Murray, "Look, that poor Indian has stolen a bicycle and doesn't know how to ride it. He is simply running away with it." Murray looked up and said, "Hey, that looks like my bike" and so we gave chase. We caught him and led him to the police station. We reported the incident to the authorities. They smiled, and took down the information. As we left the front door of the station, we saw the thief trotting out of the backdoor. The law said, 'Well, gentlemen, you have your bike."

I soon learned about the law in that other America. The system is quite elaborate and complicated. One is amazed at all the laws and pretended authority. We were always having to get some kind of legal stamp of approval for almost everything. There are often long delays to get that signature of approval to do some simple task. Yet, despite the wait, one knows that the authority is not busy, often sitting at his desk with every indication that he is taking a siesta.

Although Lorla's sewing machine had been purchased and used in the States for a year, it did look "new" and was so classified in Bolivia and import taxes had to be paid on a new machine. On the other hand, when we went back to Lima in

1951 and took a new washing machine with us, we thoughtfully washed some old oily rags and left the "dirty ring around the collar." This we were able to import as "used."

We had been in Bolivia a couple of months when I received a tax bill requiring payment of a tax on all electrical appliances we owned, retroactive for a year. I said, "But I have been here only three months." "That doesn't matter, you must pay for the entire calendar year." He was very convincing, especially when he could speak in his native language, and I was still just a beginner.

Laws are very interesting in that other America. A decree in Bolivia required that all property owners place galvanized gutters on their dwellings or pay a "multa" or fine. We were sure that there were not enough gutters in the entire country to put those gutters on those adobe tile roofed buildings. It was more convenient to pay the fine. Another good decree required all to paint their buildings before the national holidays. It certainly made a spectaular difference to see all those dwellings spruced up even if only the front received the required coat of paint. Maybe we could try it for the 4th of July some year, or every year?

"¿Qué me importa la ley?" Many are asking that question here today as it relates to our own criminal justice system.

19

ACCORDING TO THE RULES

Our mission school in Callao, Peru, was well known for its high educational standards. One of our students, Octavio Roman, had been enrolled to improve his English. He seemed to show promise and was also advised to take further studies at the U.S. Cultural Institute, in Lima, a program sponsored by the U.S. embassy. He was a good student and a personable young man. He was granted a scholarship to study at the University of Nebraska in Lincoln. He was told that he could not take gainful employment while there under the scholarship grant. I told him to be sure to follow those rules and he understood.

He went to the United States early in order to get acclimated and to become familiar with the area. Since he arrived early he discovered that the Nebraska State Fair was in session and they were looking for people to work there. This was or seemed like an excellent opportunity to get some additional pocket money. His English was good enough and the temptation to get a little extra money was too great. He took a job forgetting the rules until he got his Social Security card. He wrote me a letter, and expressed his fear of expulsion from the U.S. before he had even begun his studies. I told him to contact some friends of mine in Lincoln, asking for their help. With their assistance and his promise to behave himself he was able to get the matter straightened out and the dilemma resolved. From then on he followed the rules and was able to continue his studies at the University. Years later, I learned that his son had also secured a scholarship to continue his studies at the same university.

Another one of our top students was Pablo Gushiken. His mother, a U.S. citizen from Hawaii, but of Japanese descent, asked me to help her son get a scholarship in the U.S. I said I would speak to friends at the U.S. Consulate and embassy, which I did. They didn't offer much encouragement. It was war time. Meanwhile I went back to the U.S. for a furlough. Upon returning to Peru I learned that somehow Pablo had managed to get through the requirements and had secured a scholarship, and was already in the U.S. studying at a university there. The Gushikens were exceedingly grateful, giving me undue credit for arranging the whole matter for them when all I had done was to make an inquiry at the U.S. embassy.

Somehow both of them managed to meet the requirements according to the rules. It was nice to get the "undeserved credit."

A FRIEND INDEED?

I went to the Argentine consul's office in New York in 1961 to request information about the requirements needed to return to Argentina as a resident. I was given a typewritten sheet of the many things I would need. I was a bit surprised by the rather long list: certificate of good health, certificate from the police that I had no record, a statement from the bank that I had funds, etc. One of the employees saw me and recognized me. I questioned the list of requirements, and he thought he was doing me a favor when he said, "You don't need all those things. We know you. Your office is over on Tucumán. You have your birth certificates and proof that you lived there before. That is all you will need." I thanked him and took him at his word and sailed merrily back to Buenos Aires.

Immigration officers from Argentina boarded our ship in Montevideo for the overnight passage to Buenos Aires and proceeded to check that the passengers had the necessary documents needed before disembarking. I was again shown that long list of requirements. I had our birth certificates, our marriage certificate, passport, and birth certificates for the girls. The officials on board requested the other items on the list. We spent half the night looking through our things to find something that would satisfy them. And where was that legalized wedding certificate with all those golden official seals? When that was produced, they said the marriage certificate did not indicate any children. What to do? The friend who knew me was back in New York. I tried to explain that we had no children when we were married and therefore they were not on the original certificate.

It was good that I spoke Spanish well. They seemed to understand and believed me when I said I would contact a friend in the U.S. and get the necessary documents updated to show the births of the children. They did allow me to disembark. They could not keep me on the boat. I did write and secured one of the fanciest and most beautiful marriage certificates one could imagine. It took a few weeks to get all that done, and by then I felt like I was one of the most legal and legitimate residents of the country. I continued to go about my business normally. From that experience I learned to follow the rules and to be prepared with all the documents needed—plus a few extra.

FRIENDS

In Latin America much importance was placed on friendship. These friends were often used to accomplish one's own purposes. In fact, one could do almost anything if he had the right friends or, as we might say, "connections." I would sometimes call on a friend who had a friend who could help ease the laborious task of up-dating one's carnet or cedula, or of getting some item cleared through customs. One could accomplish almost anything if one had the right friends or knew the right people. It all seemed a part of the way of life to cultivate the friends who could secure favors.

On one occasion a friend in the U.S. was concerned about the whereabouts of her brother and his wife who were making a trip by jeep to South America. She hadn't heard from her brother for weeks and was quite worried. She knew they had reached Ecuador, since she had heard they had been bogged down on some of the muddy roads in that country. One of the parents of children in our Victoria School in the 1950s had a relative who had a government position which dealt with foreigners coming through Peru. I asked him to help me locate this couple. He was not only able but gave me a daily report about their whereabouts, telling me when they reached the Peruvian border, and then a daily progress report until I had them safe in our home. The friend was a friend in deed. I did warn the couple not to try to travel the Pan American highway again until we had news of its completion.

Although it is too easy and usually inaccurate to generalize, I think I agree with the common opinions that our South American friends tend to be somewhat explosive at times—striking like a "fósforo" or match. They may seem to flare up in anger briefly, but that flame usually burns out quickly and the matter seems to be over and forgotten. There is always jealousy in any culture. I am sure that there must have been some long lasting feuds and family grudges, but they seemed to be infrequent.

I was told of a lad in Buenos Aires who was a "lustrabotas" (shoe shine boy) who had made friends with a North American visiting down there. The lad had seen movies and had met many North Americans, so he readily accepted when this friend offered him a trip to the United States. The boy went to the U.S and stayed for a couple of months. When he returned to his own country, he was asked how he liked the U.S. Did he like it there? The lad thought for a moment and then said, "Puro Gringo" (they were all "gringos"). He decided that he had seen all the gringos he wanted to see for a while and was glad to be back home with his "friends".

25

A FAVOR?

During the time we were in Argentina in the 1960s I usually drove the company Jeep station wagon which was very serviceable, but not too fancy in appearance. When some of the Executive Officers of the American Bible Society in New York were expected for a meeting in Buenos Aires, a friend who was in charge of the local Industria Kaiser Argentina office, loaned me a more comfortable passenger car to use for a few days. I was pleased with his gesture of courtesy and chauffered the visitors around.

On Sunday as I was returning from the airport, a policeman stopped me to check on the papers. He discovered that the inspection sticker on the windshield had expired and another inspection was due. In fact, he thought the car should be impounded, or worse that I should spend the night in jail. Lorla even got out of the car and was going to take a bus home.

I explained it was a company car and that I was not responsible for its registration. We spent a half hour or so discussing the matter and finally when I promised that I would see that the inspection was done on Monday, he let me go. I had convinced him that nothing could be done until the morrow anyway.

When I returned that car to the company I expressed my gratitude and told them about the overdue inspection. They thought that it was quite a joke, but I didn't especially appreciate the humor of it. I was glad that the "visiting firemen" had just returned to New York.

WHEN IN ROME?

One can make many mistakes while learning a language and the people will laugh with you and not at you. One has to be more cautious with local customs. On one occasion in Lima I was familiar with the "word" but not with what was involved. A young couple asked me if I would be "padrino" for their child. Thinking they wanted me to be a godfather and stand with them when their child was baptized, I was flattered and unwittingly said that I would and I did. Later, when the husband and father abandoned his family, I learned that custom demanded that as "padrino" I was expected to look after the special needs of the mother and child. I admit that I felt somewhat guilty for so naively accepting thcir request. I hope and pray that the mother and child are doing well.

As a pastor of the La Florida church, in Lima, I was officiating at a wedding. All was going very well until the little lad who had been given the task of carrying the wedding ring on a neatly adorned pillow had no idea what had happened to it, and since the best man had no solution, we proceeded with the nuptials as though everything was in order. One must not lose face. When the ceremony was completed the problem was revealed. The procession had walked through the grass to get to the chapel and the ring had evidently fallen during that time. It was like looking for a needle in a haystack. After a lengthy search, the ring was found, and several exclaimed "¡Qué milagro!" (What a miracle!) I called it good luck.

It was a typical expression, "¡Qué Milagro!" Anything a little out of the ordinary is called a miracle. I happened to run across a fellow I hadn't seen for a while. His greeting was "¡Qué milagro que tu estás aquí!" (What a miracle that you are here!). To me it was simply a happenstance. I did not see that there was anything miraculous about it. I noticed that the Latin Americans often tried to make anything out of the ordinary as miraculous. It was an expression repeated frequently, rather than one to be taken literally.

The people in that other America seemed to place a lot of importance on one's fate or destiny. If I had a flat tire, it was my fate or destiny. It was meant to be. I had the impression that it is more common in South America for people to accept what they call "destino." Something happens either favorable or unfavorable, and with a casual shrug of the shoulders many will say, "Pués, es el destino." (It is fate.) Just accept fate and carry on as best you can. Of course, our friends to the south don't have a monopoly on the expression, but it just seems to be more readily acceptable in that area. The song "Qué será, será" (What will be, will be) became popular in North America some years ago.

The word "simpático" is used frequently, yet it is difficult to define. It is used to describe one who has a pleasing personality. A happy child with a nice smile might be said to be "muy simpático." We might call it personality plus. Yet it is often expressed on first meeting of a person, before "personality" has had time to be judged. It is not only a pleasing appearance, but might also mean a person who is pleasant and nice, someone who indicates a willingness to do something for you beyond the call of duty.

There are so many things to learn in another culture.

"¡QUÉ PAQUETE!"

"¡Qué paquete!" is frequently used in referring to a person with a nice figure. We might say, "Well built," or "stacked." What I have in mind, though, is our custom of packaging.

I wanted to eat some crackers with a bowl of soup. Those crackers were so well packed and sealed that I had to use a knife and scissors to get to them. I know that we must assure cleanliness, freshness and sanitation by thorough packaging but my soup was almost cold by the time I got to the crackers. Perhaps the solution is to eat croutons, or reheat the soup.

I kept thinking of the difference when buying crackers in much of South America. In Lima, I used to go down to the corner grocery to buy a kilo of crackers. The clerk would tear off a sheet of the morning's or yesterday's newspaper, open it up, and then take a handful or two of crackers, out of a barrel, fold over the newspaper and I was on my way to take my crackers home. That system was used for many articles. Sometimes one carried a little string bag to use for carrying more than one such "wrapped" package.

I recall that bakers sometimes made very large loaves of bread with very thick crusts. These thick crusts served as a wrapping only. It didn't matter who or how many people touched it, or if it fell on the floor or ground. This crust was all sliced or cut away, so a person would have nice clean bread for making sandwiches, but without the "cáscara" or crust. I didn't appreciate that system, either, because in some instances the crust was about the best part of the bread.

I return again to the extreme caution of packaging in the United States. I imagine that we spend as much money in expertly and exquisitely packing merchandise than many countries actually spend on the product itself. I am not in the marketing or merchandising business but I think that we often overdo it.

I used to buy bananas at the markets in South America by the "hand" rather than by the pound. Actually here I think we here are being fairer since it depends on the size of the fruit. Five small bananas can hardly compare with five large ones.

When one went to the market to buy meat, one did not expect to find prepacked plastic packages. The meat cuts were different, and despite arguments to the contrary, it is still difficult to find much better beef than the "lomos" and “asados” of Argentine beef, in spite of the grass fed cattle. I could go to the market and buy a whole tenderloin, wrapped loosely in a piece of newspaper and at a very reasonable price. Above all, I could afford to buy it and enjoy it. I can still see those Argentine construction workers on the streets of Buenos Aires during the noon hours barbecuing a huge chunk of meat on an iron bar over an open fire. I can't argue the quality of their workmanship, but I can certainly appreciate the quality of their eating. They can be justifiably proud of their well known "asados." My taste buds still get aroused when I think of a delicious "bife de lomo, puré de papas and ensalada mixta and a glass of Mendocino."

(Tenderloin, mashed potatoes, tossed salad, and a glass of wine.)

While in Buenos Aires I knew the manager of the Rockefeller financed and developed supermarkets which were being introduced in the 1960s. I had the temerity to go shopping on the opening day of one of them. It was quite an experience. I learned that the shoppers didn't know how to push those carts around without banging into each other. My ankles and the backs of my legs were battered and bruised from the experience. I spoke to Mr. Boogart, the manager of the stores when twenty were in operation. He said that just as in the U.S. the rate of pilferage was high, not so much from the customers but from suppliers and truckers. I suppose that it is part of the price of progress.

I have never had a course in marketing, and I am aware of the importance of neatness and attractiveness in packaging, but I still get a bit frustrated when it takes me so long to unwrap something. Much is done to save time and for the question of cleanliness, but I prefer to let most of the ready-mixes refer to concrete. My motto would be more availability and accessibility and a little less sealed packaging.

ANOTHER PACKAGE

I had a young pastor in Lima who seemed quite promising, was intelligent and who had a good personality. As a District Superintendent I sent him to Trujillo in northern Peru to develop a church and to work with university students in that area. A year or two later I secured a scholarship for him to study in the United States. He was delighted at the opportunity, even though his wife and sons could not go with him. Some time after he left a young lady came into my office with a baby in her arms. I was pleased to see the little creature, but I was shocked when she exclaimed "You are responsible!" I hardly knew the girl, so I asked, "What do you mean?"

"Well," she said, "you sent a young man to work with the students where I met him and he is the father." I was nonplussed that I should be accused of being responsible for the child. I really didn't feel all that guilty, but something had to be done. I talked to the wife of the young man who was soon to return from the States. She was very forgiving and understanding and generously offered to take the baby as part of her own family. I soon learned of the strength of the mother. She would not give up her child to the young man's wife. I had created a dilemma. I promised that I would help her find a job, and she agreed to leave the child with her parents while she worked.

Sometime later, I received a call from a friend who was in charge of a school in Paraguay.

He said he had given a job to the young man who had just returned from the U.S. and was having problems with him. I asked, "What is he teaching?" My friend said, "He is teaching civic and moral education." I replied, "Well, he has a good background and knows the subject!" He was dismissed and went to Brazil and after a time to the U.S where he still is as far as I know. For the life of me I still can't feel that I was responsible for that baby, and I assume that both the mother and baby are doing well.

MACHISMO

It always seemed strange to me that many men in the other America seemed to want to support more than one family. Frankly, I don't know how they did it either socially or financially. In North America it seems to be done differently either with mistresses or with a series of marriages. Both ways would seem to be rather expensive and somewhat out of line with traditional values.

We have adopted the word "macho" in North America as the "in" thing when all the word means is "male", We assume that macho means "muy macho" (very male). Now it seems that via television and the movies machismo has become a part of North American culture (or lack of it) and we are trying to make more of it than originally intended by thc meaning of the word. I don't see that much difference in being very male or very “hembra" (female). In that other America women were just as female as in any other area. They did not seem to mind "flaunting" it. They would dress nicely in order to be seen and appreciated by both sexes.

Men had a great facility with clever little sayings or expressions called "piropos" which they used to say to women. They were often well planned and rehearsed before being attempted. Then the man would tell by the woman's reaction or response if she was interested in pursuing the matter. They were very open about the use of their eyes and were masters of body language.

Undressing with the eyes was a very noticeable phase of their methods. I can't recall of having read of any litigation over the question of harrassment. I felt that the women there would have missed the "piropos", which made them feel young and attractive. It seemed that the whole attitude in these matters was much more relaxed than that commonly seen in the United States. It also seemed that the women were much more tolerant of any marital indiscretions by their husbands.

We were often surprised by irregular relationships. For example, our neighbor across the street had a wife and two children. Our children played together. We were rather taken aback one night in a meeting in another part of the city, when a woman we knew introduced us to her husband. It was our neighbor from across the street. In spite of seeming marital irregularities there seemed to be a family loyalty among the children. The oldest would struggle to get an education and a good job. Then each member in turn would help a younger member to get through school in order to find an equal opportunity for success.

Divorce, of course, was illegal, so many other things were done. I was somewhat astounded when one of the presidents asked that his marriage be annulled so he could marry his young secretary, especially after he and his wife of so many years had been blessed with numerous grandchildren.

Our "liberated" North American female probably thinks that most women in the other America don't know the meaning of freedom and that they are less advanced than in the U.S. Still in both Americas life goes on. People seem to enjoy life. Families are raised. There are both understandings and misunderstandings within the whole concept of gender. "Viva el amor" and may the matter of human relations bring better understanding. May each gender find the place in which it is most comfortable and respected.

NATURALLY LEGITIMATE

A newly arrived colleague and his wife had a baby and I knew that it should be registered within five days. I told him about that requirement. He wanted to be independent, and when he did go to register the child about a week later, it was registered as a "natural" rather than a "legitimate" baby. As a result he had to hire a lawyer and spend several months getting the child properly registered as a legitimate son.

A child born out of wedlock in Peru was known as a natural child, which is much better than calling the child illegitimate. Why make a child bear the title and stigma since he had little to do with the situation?

Now with the growing number of teenage mothers and often unknown or uncertain fathers in North America, some similar arrangement may have to be made. Natural or legitimate, the real question is who is to care for and pay the expenses for rearing the child. Hopefully we can find a more human and humane approach to the question of child bearing and support.

PETTY THIEVERY

In any area in which there is a vast discrepancy between the haves and have-nots as in Peru, petty thievery is almost certain to be commonplace. Someone had to work long and hard hours to steal a lock off our metal gate in front of the house. It had to have taken him a lot of time and work to remove that lock. Still he would probably have had to work for a month to get the money he received from selling the lock he had stolen. On that same night thieves broke into the Escuela America in La Victoria. This mission school of nearly 800 students, was an elementary school in a poorer section of Lima. The thieves had taken the clocks from each classroom. A guard sleeping in the building said he heard nothing. I didn't know why cat burglars would want clocks. They also took typewriters and some cash from our bookstore as well as some school uniforms. The main expense and inconvenience was to replace the two large front doors of the school.

Another night the main locks were stolen off the doors of a church while the congregation was at worship inside and no one heard a thing.

John Shappell, one of my colleagues and Director of our school in Callao, did have his car stolen one Saturday evening while he had gone to a theater. There was no car-jacking and the thieves were considerate enough to return and park the stolen car in back of the school, minus the four wheels, but the vehicle was easy to find and no other serious damage was done.

A special type of lock was designed to lock the wheels to the car and to lock the spare wheel in the trunk. It was somewhat annoying to carry windshield wipers in one's pocket to avoid theft. That was more of an inconvenience than a real loss.

One day in Cochabamba some things were missing in the dormitory, and after some thought it was decided to call the police. They came and asked, "Who did it?" and then proceeded to take all the servants into custody. We were deprived of their help for three or four days. We never found out "who did it" or recovered the missing items. Lorla had a favorite pair of scissors which she had brought from the U.S. They were ball-bearing so were continually sharpening as they were being used. These were left on the table one night and were gone the next morning.

One did begin to feel a little uneasy wondering what would disappear next, but at least there were no shootings or stabbings. No one was killed or even injured. We chalked it up as a learning experience from someone who was in desperate need and who had no welfare assistance, food or other type of help to rely upon.

Two of our girls' bikes disappeared during the afternoon from the back of the house in Acassuso, Buenos Aires during a time when the River Plate, two blocks away was in a state of flood, and people were displaced and roaming the streets. We should have taken precautions. The girls thought their loss was of such magnitude it could in no way be considered as "petty thievery."

SCHOOL DAYS

My first experience in educational work in South America was as a teacher in the secondary section of the Instituto Americano in Cochabamba. When for health reasons, I was transferred to Lima, Peru in 1946, I was named Director of our mission school, Escuela America, in La Victoria which at that time had over 800 students. Needless to say at first I felt like a fish out of water until the staff offered their total support and dedication to what we were doing in our program. The mayor of the city had his sons in our school, and that was a good endorsement.

Our student body consisted of representatives of several ethnic groups. Most were "mestizos." Others were almost pure Indian. A high percentage were black. There were also some orientals. The school was very popular, and the demand far exceeded the room we had. We had to turn away at least five or six students for each one we accepted. We also offered scholarships to needy and excellent or superior students. We were always overcrowded.

The teachers in the school had been there for years, and I was the youngest and a Gringo. I sometimes wonder how I was able to hold their loyalty and respect, since I know that I could not have done the job they were doing. I was reminded of the saying "Él que sabe, sabe. Él que no sabe, es el jefe." (He who knows, knows. He who doesn't know is the boss!)

I was always amazed at the ability of some of our teachers to maintain such remarkable discipline. Lucilla Vidal, who taught kindergarten with a helper, had sixty students at long tables in one room. They sat there at attention and she maintained complete control. I was even more surprised at how much those little ones learned. They always did very well in the national tests and we rarely ever had a disciplinary problem. When a teacher walked into the room, the students stood to greet the teacher. They were extremely polite and well regimented. Even when I walked into the room, the students would all stand and say in English, "Good morning, Señor Director."

One might flinch at this sign of respect but when one sees the chaotic disorganization which seems to prevail in many U.S. schools today, one wonders how much they have to offer. The system used was at first appalling to me, but I adjusted and learned that it wasn't all bad. The students had a collection of "cuadernos" (notebooks) in which they copied their lessons the old fashioned way. Then during exams they would "back the book" and recite what they had written. I frowned upon the system but later learned that they knew much more than I had thought possible. Of course, we had to follow the curriculum prescribed by the national department of education.

The tuition fees were set by the government. The school budget was far in excess of the tuition we were allowed to charge, so other measures had to be taken. I ordered our English text books from Scott-Foresman and Ginn and Company, and the parents had to pay for them. The students had to wear uniforms, a navy blue sweater and slacks for the boys, and a navy blue sweater and skirt for the girls. These were made by a local company. Books and uniforms were sold at a profit in order to keep teachers' salaries commensurate with those paid in other private schools and to meet other expenses.

A problem which concerned me was the compliance with social laws which required not only a retirement sum of month's pay for each year of service but a pension based on years of service. Our reserves were far from sufficient to cover such a load if too many teachers retired at the same time.

One year we had a minor problem when we tried to get an area of prostitution two blocks from our school moved to another part of the city. A local magazine called "YA" supported our campaign as did our school doctor. One day orders came from a government office to cease and desist in that campaign, and we were obliged to follow their orders. This was a minor skirmish, and the school has kept going all these intervening years.

THE JUDGE

The Bolivian government appointed a board of examiners to test all students who were supposedly completing a course toward graduation. One day in 1945 I received a notice from the Department of Education asking me to be a member of the "jurado," or board of examiners for English. The note said I was supposed to report to a school run by Sisters of the Sacred Heart on a certain day at a certain hour. It sounded like an interesting assignment and besides that I knew I had no choice in the matter.

Since this was a new experience I didn't know exactly what to expect. I was cordially received by the Sisters who not only wanted to impress me, but to gain my favor so that I would give good reports on their students. I was offered a cup of coffee and welcomed to the first group of students. There were two other examiners but I was the only North American. We sat behind a large table and as the students names were called, they appeared before our table so we could judge them on their knowledge of English. As custom there dictated, the student was asked to draw a little "bolito" or number, from a box on the table and that would determine the area of the question to which they were supposed to respond. The girls, all spruced up, of course, were quite nervous, since this would decide how well they would compare with other students. I can't recall the questions but I remember one was: "What is another name for petroleum? The young lady responded, "Mineral oil." Another member of our examiners said, "correct" but I hesitated to add: "It is not necessary to say "mineral" because oil alone would have been a sufficient answer.

And then another question related to some section of literature. This has been a long time ago so I can't remember the exact question, of course, but, the young lady responded by reciting a section of information which she had memorized. She went on for at least five minutes, repeating verbatim from her notebook. They had page after page of questions and answers which the teachers had dictated and which they had memorized in "voz alta" (aloud). They were unable to answer the question directly, and had to refer back to the notebooks and repeat pages of related material, not all that pertinent. They wanted to impress the members of the panel how well they knew English. It was so different that it was difficult to judge how much English they really knew as they did not give a direct answer to the questions asked. I tried to be as courteous as I could and to give them the benefit of the doubt. I must admit that they probably could not have responded to any direct question I asked about English, but at least they had made a notebook.

These questions went on for hours as each of these young ladies tried to give some response to the questions that were asked. They had a general idea about the questions, but at times they seemed totally befuddled because of their lack of the knowledge of English.

Then after several hours of questions of

these young girls, the members of the panel were invited to have a cup of tea and refreshments. As I recall some of the Sisters were from Ireland and since they were a cloistered group they asked me all kinds of questions about world affairs, about the government in the U.S. and other interesting questions unrelated to the test itself, but curious to know what was going on outside the halls of their school It was an unusual experience.

I was also invited to see some of the work that the young ladies had supposedly done in embroidery, sewing and other handwork. I was much impressed by the quality of the work they had done, more so, for their work in sewing and embroidery, than their knowledge of English. After having spent a day with these teaching Sisters and with these young women who were eager to get some kind of acceptance for their knowledge of English, I was dismissed and returned home. I had spent an unusual day as a member of the board of examiners.

FORWARD MARCH!

We were always having "desfiles" in Bolivia. It seemed that every few days there was some kind of patriotic or religious or some other kind of holiday. The students had to have their uniforms clean and pressed, their shoes shined and line up to march somewhere. We would receive one of the frequent official decrees that we were supposed to assemble at one of the plazas. We spent a lot of time marching. We didn't have any kind of marching band, or any kind of band at all, but we marched. We would have 400-500 students from primary and secondary lined up. They had marched for a long time and one of the boys suddenly stopped and I said, "What's wrong? You are supposed to be marching." He said, "My feet and legs hurt, I am tired. I think I will have more patriotism in my legs than in my head." "That could be true, but keep on marching," I said. After a few more steps he said, "But it is affecting my rheumatism." I said, "You are too young for rheumatism. Get back in line, and keep those lines straight."

One of the problems was that it was usually warm, dry and dusty. After marching all that time they were expected to stand at attention while the speeches were being made. We would walk along the side lines and notice that some of them would begin to collapse from the heat We would help them up and ask them to stand still and keep at attention. I almost agreed with that young man when he said, he would have more patriotism in his feet than in his head.

The girls, who had to march along with the rest of the students, would get all ready. They would come back exhausted, complaining about getting so dusty from all that marching. "But it is worth it," they said, "because we have to go back down to regain control of Antofagasta. Chile. We don't have a sea port. We have to have a seaport." I said, “You haven't had one for years." “But we're going to do it,” these young ladies said. “If the young men won't do it, we will have to do it. We need to recover our seaport in Antofagasta.”

Later when I was in Antofagasta, a nice small city on the coast of Chile, I asked the people there if they were ready for the Bolivians to come and take back their seaport. Of course, they weren't sure what I was talking about, but they replied, "Take back, certainly not. We are not ready for anyone to come take over our port." The Bolivians would be regarded more like intruders because they had been separated for so long that the Chileans no longer remembered they had once been together. The young ladies had not given it much thought. They were just being patriotic.

A big event was Mother's day, "Día da la Madre." All the students, dressed up in their best uniforms had to march out to the hill. It took a long time to get there. They marched and marched, not always in perfect file. They had to stand at attention for an hour on a rather warm day and some of the students suffered from heat prostration. One of the boys said, "Well, I'm not sure my mother would really appreciate my being out here like this to do her honor. She would probably find something else for me to do which would be more helpful to her."

We were in Cochabamba during V-Day too, when the war in Europe ended and to show our support and celebration for the great V Day event, all the students and teachers were required to march first of all down to the main plaza or square and to stand at attention with all the students from other schools. To us this was a momentous event, but required standing for a long time. The speeches by the ambassadors and consuls of the Allied countries were long, sometimes enthusiastic, but much of the time quite boring for those children. And then, of course, they all had to march back to the school.

We had to have special programs in our school to celebrate patriotic events. It was instructive occasionally. The objective was to have these historical facts indelibly engraved on their minds as well as events in the world which they hoped they would always remember, especially at quiz time.

At the beginning of each school day before classes started, all the students had to assemble and stand at attention. After a word of greeting to the principal of the school, they sang the national anthem and the pledge of allegiance to their country was given. Then somebody would usually have a poem ready to recite about loyalty and patriotism or about some military hero. They memorized material from their "cuadernos" which had been dictated previously by the teachers. On special days, we would have a guest such as the mayor or some governmental figure, who would come to speak to the group. This was a required assembly and they were quite accustomed to this kind of patriotic observance. They didn't complain, although I admit that I got bored from time to time because it seemed a bit repetitious and, for me, it began to lose some of its meaning or significance. And yet they did remember. They could recite a great deal of material about the great heroes of their country. Perhaps we in the United States have gone to the other extreme. I sometimes wonder about this patriotism.

One day we were talking about all this marching. They had gone visiting to another school and heard a new song. One of the boys said, "I did not know that we were marching to Zion. Where is it?"

CRUISING: OLD STYLE

A Spanish forerunner of today's cruising was called a promenade. Each town in that other America had its own plaza or park in the center of town. I was amused to find a "sloth" hanging from the trees in the plaza in Cochabamba. These plazas were always filled, and the young ladies with their chaperones (usually their mother, an aunt, or an older woman) would walk around the square in one direction. The young men would walk around in the opposite direction, stealing glances at the young ladies as they walked by. They would size up the young women perhaps with a wink to show their approval. The young woman would coyly somehow give her approval and a desire for further meetings.

As I recall these promenades were usually done on Friday or Sunday evenings, but might occur at any time. Some of the men would take the diagonal path across the square in order to see the "girl" again without waiting for the entire revolution. Since I never participated in one I was never sure how they succeeded so well. By their glances and signs the boys and girls made their wishes known. Both parties would be sure to join the promenade each week until further contacts could be established. Men ogle the women and women are just as accustomed to staring or observing as the male.

Many of our mission secondary schools in South America were coeducational. This was contrary to local custom. We were able to prove that it could work satisfactorily and naturally. We even introduced the idea of having all day "paseos" or picnics. There was careful vigilance by the teachers who kept the girls and boys walking the whole time except when they sat down to have their picnic lunch. By keeping them on the move during the all day hike through the countryside there was little time for problems to arise. In spite of the close supervision by the teachers who had to walk along, both the boys and girls seemed to enjoy these excursions, since they could at least walk with some of the opposite sex. They knew they had to obey the rules, and we knew they knew the rules.

I understand that our mission schools were first started in Bolivia at the invitation of the government and some of the graduates in time occupied positions of leadership in the country including the office of the presidency. There was always a demand to get into our schools. After further training, some of our students would return to teach in them.

GO TEAM, GO!

The people in the South American countries really enjoy sports activities and contests. Not too long ago the U.S. hosted the world cup of "futbol." We here had difficulty understanding why the large crowds who came from that other America were so excited about some of those games which sometimes seemed boring to many people in the U.S. because we haven't developed much enthusiasm for the game of soccer (futbol). We like the kind of drag down, knock them out contact, rather than the finesse and technique of the game which soccer requires.

Actually you have probably noticed that not only have the other countries of the world learned the game of basketball which was a U.S. invention, but some are playing it quite well. Occasionally some of these countries defeat us at our own game. Some of the players are bought up by some of our professional national leagues.

My introduction to sport contests was in our school in Cochabamba where we tried to have a basketball team that could play the faculty. I noticed that our school team did not know all the elemental factors of the game of basketball. I tried to help the coach introduce some new ideas in preparing plays rather than just to run and shoot, although I have nothing against that style, either, as many of our big league players are playing that type of individual game.

Some of the schools in Cochabamba decided to have a championship in which each school would participate and then at the end of the season see which team had won the most games during the year. The only trouble was that they had never had that kind of a competition before. It seemed that when one school lost a game, they thought they had had it and wouldn't play any more. Why play if you couldn't win? That was the general attitude. As a result it seemed that the city championship was determined as much by default as in actual contest. LaSalle, a Catholic school and our main rival, quit after they were beaten by our mission school. They wouldn't play any more. That wasn't a good lesson in sportsmanship. We had to work on that for a long time so they would play for the whole season, win or lose, and let the winner be determined at the end of the season.

In all of South America, sports are taken very seriously. I went to a "futbol" game once in which the national team of Bolivia was playing the national team of another country. I think it was Argentina. It was a very serious and hotly contested game. And since it was a game of such consequence, they had brought in the referee from another country and brought him in by helicopter and deposited him on the field. At the end of the game the helicopter reappeared, picked him up, and took him out of the arena for his own safety. I thought that the interesting thing was that his name was Lynch. He probably realized that in order to avoid such a fate for himself he had better exit while he had a good chance. I don't know if they ever had any lynching of a referee, but I'm sure some of the people were excited enough at the time that they would have had at least a secret desire to do just that.

I was impressed by the fact that there were such huge stadiums, in Argentina and Brazil in particular, seating 100,000 people or more. Team sport fanatics filled those stadiums to capacity week after week during the entire season. It seemed that these contests were almost like religious rituals to them and they were very loyal fans. Emotion ran high. I recall once at River Plate how the people in the upper decks would take their newspapers and set them on fire and drop them over the edge of their section down on the people in a lower section who might not agree with the way the game was going. It was exciting, but I thought a bit dangerous to have those flames drifting down over one's head. It seemed that every person was a "hincha" or fan of one particular club or another and there were intense rivalries. At least the games seemed to be almost like an international conflict. I remember one time after seeing an exhibition of a futbol game that afternoon I saw a crowd of men gathered around the church. They were arguing the merits and plays of the game and were almost to the point of fisticuffs. When they seemed to get so excited over a football game, it was almost like a mini-war.

In Peru I was a "hincha" of Universitarios and our main rival was Alianza Lima. I was not quite so dedicated in my support since Alianza Lima did provide us with facilities for our athletic program for the school in La Victoria. I still remember how excited they got when their team had won a large victory or how depressed they became when their team happened to lose. I've heard since that they have even introduced their own type of "wave" among the fans. I haven't been there yet to become a part of that scene, but I would be fearful of that wave becoming a tide instead of just moving from side to side.

There was another kind of sport which did not thrill me that much, and that was bullfighting, which they seemed to enjoy very much. The bull fights were called runs or "corridas." As they began to taunt the bull until the bull became very angry, I began to feel more support for the bull than for the bullfighter. It was not an even fight as far as I was concerned. Of course, that is a gringo interpretation. To me the worst part was when they had to kill the bull and would have to stab the bull several times before completing the job. Occasionally, of course, the bull does win and gores the toreador. A spectacular stab done correctly and cleanly with the collapse of the bull would bring cheers of "Olé!" At the end the notorious toreador would be given an ear for his skill, and for a spectacular appearance, he would receive the tail of the animal. But to me having to go through that six times in an afternoon was too much of an overkill.

ON TIME?

Generally speaking our friends in Latin America are not as concerned about time as most of the rest of us. Being a bit tardy is to be expected. It could be embarrassing if one arrives on time and the hosts are not expecting one just yet. They did adjust graciously if the gringos awkwardly arrived on time. I had to ask if the time agreed was "hora inglesa" (English time), the exact time.

Something a little unusual did occur at a funeral service. The hearse had brought the deceased on time and the driver said that he would be back in half an hour to make the trip to the cemetery. The service was over, the pallbearers carried the coffin out to the sidewalk, but alas there was no hearse. The pallbearers stood there feeling the weight on their shoulders, a weight which increased as time went by. Finally, a U.S. military representative, backed up with a truck and asked the pallbearers to put the coffin on the truck and we all left for the cemetery. The hearse arrived about two hours later. The officer and I were already back from the interment The officer said, "I am not in any hurry to go, but I hope when my time comes, that the hearse arrives on time, since my truck and I won't be here to offer our services."

On one occasion Lorla and I were to take a trip by train from Cochabamba. We arrived a little early to be sure of catching our train. We were shocked to see the train waiting and ready to pull out. When we inquired, we learned that we were about to take yesterday's train which was just about 24 hours late. To be on what we thought was the safe side, we decided to take that late train. We hoped that it would get us to our destination on time. Today's train caught up with us about four hours later, and so everyone was "on time."

One day I was asked to perform a wedding. It was just a little past time for the nuptials. The church was full. The organist had played the appropriate music. The bride and bridesmaids were all ready and waiting. The little flower girl and ring bearer were fidgeting. All was ready except the groom. As time went by, the bride and her attendants were weeping. The organist played for an hour. I was about to announce that due to unforeseen circumstances the wedding would be postponed until further notice. At that moment, the groom and best man came charging into the church. The excuse was, "It was almost impossible to get a cab." The wedding ceremony was completed a little later. Does time matter?

I had looked forward to the inauguration and use of my new mahogany desk and filing cabinet in Cochabamba. The carpenter assured me that he would have everything ready in a couple of weeks. I waited for three weeks before inquiring. A month went by without any news. Two months passed, then three. Finally, one day, I was surprised when the carpenter arrived in his little truck and jubilantly told of the fine job he had done in preparing such beautiful furniture. I could only join in his pleasure and happiness. I was delighted to at last have the furniture I had ordered so long ago.

In Buenos Aires I requested the installation of a telephone in our house in Acassuso so that we would not have to inconvenience our neighbor. A year went by, then two, and I had almost forgotten that I had requested one. The day came when a young man appeared saying he had my telephone and asked where I wanted it installed. I remembered that a space had been left to place the phone on the second floor, a pipe had been inserted to facilitate the installation of wires near my office. The telephone man said, "But, Señor, I don't have a ladder." I told him to bring the phone and put it wherever he could. He put it just inside the living room door. He promised to come back with an extension "mañana" (tomorrow). I did not want to wait for another year and asked a friend to come and put in an extension for me. Every time it rained he would have to come and "fix" it.

On one occasion a young couple from up in the mountains in Peru was staying with us in Lima for a while. The wife was expecting to deliver her baby and wanted to be in the city and closer to the hospital. One morning they reported that they thought her time was near and asked me to take her to the hospital in my car. I asked if I would have time to eat my breakfast. A few minutes later the father came running into the room to say that I should hurry. We drove at full speed to the hospital. It was nerve wracking. We got to the hospital, and the attendants there seeing our plight came running out with a gurney. The healthy baby boy was born before they arrived at the delivery room. He simply could not wait for "mañana".

"MAÑANA"

North Americans have often spoken of South America as the land of "mañana." It seems that Time is less important there. In North America we make plans and get things done in a hurry. I think that may be much less true today.

For example, I have had to have some medical treatment in the past few months here in the United States. Perhaps you may have noticed the amount of time required, not for surgery or treatment, but rather, that which is spent in waiting rooms of doctors' offices? The "médicos" are overwhelmed by the number of patients required to help them make ends meet, but the poor patient may become bored by the amount of time spent sitting in waiting rooms while reading old magazines.

The only alternative seems to be to keep a healthy diet, do aerobics, walk a lot, and if possible do your jogging. The other alternative is to die young and to do one's waiting while "pushing up daisies."

REVOLUTION OR ASSASSINATION?

In years gone by I recall having heard jokes about "Pop gun" revolutions in that other America. Actually, various attempts at revolutions occurred while we were in South America and they were very serious matters. They were usually organized by the Army or the Navy, by one or more Generals, who perhaps wanted a turn in command. Members of the same family might find themselves on opposite sides. In the United States, we pride ourselves on the orderly transfer of power, the result of the vote by the people. When an assassination of the President of the United States occurs, it is usually by the hand of one man, on whom the guilt may be placed, correctly or incorrectly. The peoples of those other lands then call us assassins. The matter was just handled differently.

My first introduction to the revolutionary outbreaks was in Bolivia when shortly after our arrival in 1945, a revolution or "golpe de estado" occurred in La Paz. It didn't affect us much in Cochabamba but President Gualberte Villaroel was slain in La Paz and his body was strung up on a lamp post in Plaza Murillo for all to see. While Lorla was in our mission hospital in Obrajes, La Paz, following this "golpe," a shot was heard. Then it was disclosed that a wounded partisan in the hospital was kept under armed guard by a soldier in the hallway. Somehow this guard managed to "shoot" his own foot.

In Peru, these periods of discontent would grow in intensity until one would read in the newspaper that the national President had gone to a mass said for his continued health and well-being. That would be an indication that the government was a bit shaky and one could expect another military leader to assume control, assured that the president had feathered his own nest sufficiently and it was now another's turn to have his share of wealth and pelf.

One Saturday morning I was in downtown Lima to go to the Post Office and to do some shopping. I had parked the car in the Plaza de Armas right in front of the Presidential Palace and had walked about four or five blocks to a quality grocery store known as 'The Hole in the Wall". They carried many imported items. They were somewhat expensive but one was assured of good products. I was just completing my purchases when we heard shouts from the street. "¡Revolución!" and "Saquéo." The owner of the store immediately began to pull down the large metal door at the front of the store. "Everyone get out or you'll have to stay inside." I thought if I stayed I could eat, but then I thought of the family back at the house and of my car, parked, of all places, down by the palace. I took the latter choice and with my bag of groceries started running back to the Plaza de Armas to get to the car. I could hear rifle fire, but I kept running. When I got to the car the traffic was one massive congestion, cars running the wrong way on one way streets. I kept going in any direction I could to get away from downtown and luckily I was able to get home. There they had heard nothing, since radio transmissions had been stopped.

I still needed to buy more groceries, so I ran down to the corner grocery store operated by a Chinese friend. All was quiet there. They knew nothing. He sold me the groceries I wanted, and then he closed his store, too. That revolution just lasted a couple of days and a new government of "militares" took over. One learned to live with those uncertainties, never knowing when one would come.

In Buenos Aire, during the sixties, we would suddenly hear communiques from the "Reds" and the "Blues" on the radio and we would know there was another struggle for power. One day Dr. Harry B. Yeatts and I were on our way to the golf course when the radio went silent. We discovered the barriers were down at the railroad crossings, but no train was in sight. Dr. Yeatts, got out of the car, raised the barrier, while I drove across the track, let the barrier back down and we went merrily on our way. The fighting was in another part of the city.

In September, 1962, I called Lorla to caution her about going to a meeting in the downtown area. The radio stations were operating normally so she went to the meeting without incident. The next day things had worsened, but I went to work as usual. The radio reported that the Chief of the Military Forces had not resigned, nor the generals under his control. They were still in power. One of our staff called in to say she could not get to work because the bridges were raised and the trains were not running. There were tanks stationed everywhere and there were troop movements. I went home after lunch and found the streets almost deserted. Businesses were closed. Commniques over the radio gave conflicting reports. One could hear orders being given by one side and then the other, requests would be heard not to cut off power to certain hospitals. It was like having a play by play account of a baseball or football game. There was never a report on the number of casualties, but we found the whole event quite exciting.

We learned to take the threats of revolution or "golpes de estado" in stride, but we were glad that we were never in the line of fire.

POLITICS

The people in the South American countries took their politics and political intervention very seriously. I was told to stay out of their political infighting since I was a foreigner and to let them settle their differences.

While in Lima, I recall a newspaper item about a charge of "nepotism" against the governor of one of the provinces in northern Peru. His defense was simply, "Well, whom can I trust better in positions of power and leadership than my own family and friends?" He was probably right, since the degree of trust was rather limited and "palabra de honor" (word of honor) had little significance. His was not an isolated case and I hear that some of that same offense can be found in the U.S as well.

I had little contact with these officials, but Enrique Peñaranda in Bolivia and Odría Amoretti in Peru had many relatives who had been connected with our work. I did have the privilege of meeting Sr. Haya de la Torre who was the founder of the APRISTA party, a Populist group which was not in power at that time. Mr. Haya de la Torre had sought refuge and was enjoying asylum in the Colombian embassy on Avenida Arequipa in Lima.

We are usually very proud of our near pure democracy in North America although with the constant friction between personal and party interests in the U.S. we are aware that congressional gridlock and personal avarice obstruct the smooth operation of government. When each seems to succumb to personal and party interest and an attitude of "let the country go hang," we realize that we are far from the political or governmental utopia which a few extreme idealists may think we have achieved

The recent election in the U.S. after months of campaign seemed rather dull and boring. Elections in that other America are held on a Sunday and everyone in the country who is eligible is required to vote. In order to avoid this, people who had dual citizenship would make it a point to be out of the country on election day. There could be twenty to thirty political parties contending for recognition and victory. It was no wonder that there was political instability.

The common idea in Peru was that the Limeños (people of Lima) are more docile and submissive. They take the disruptions in stride. It is said that in Arequipa people would not ask "Who is fighting now?" but rather "Against whom are *we* fighting this time?"

One day I was asked to assist in getting a political prisoner released. I went to the U.S Embassy to report the case but was informed to stay clear of the matter. About a week later the man was released, and the family gave me credit for something I did not do. I had their lasting gratitude anyway.

I feared for the safety of some of our friends.

One lady reported that her husband was in hiding, so her son was taken as hostage. She feared for him, since he had a mild case of tuberculosis and a lengthy stay in prison could be harmful to his health.

Everyone talks about politics in Peru, but not many can do much about these changes. The oligarchy of the military, the landed gentry, the large number of university students, and the church are the real decision makers in control of the country.

Each country in that other America has its own set of values and all are striving to live as well and harmoniously as possible. All seem to be searching for a deeper meaning of life, liberty and the pursuit of happiness in somewhat different ways at times. North America is probably a little more technologically advanced, but there are many values through which life can be assessed. I once visited Jorge Luis Borges, the Argentine writer. He was in his declining years, almost totally blind. He was very bilingual, and the conversation revealed that he had a good understanding and appreciation of life in both Americas. In over a score of years in that other America I think I learned a little but realize that I am not sure how things ought to be. I am sure there are no absolute answers for the futures of the two Americas. Our goals are still elusive in the North as well as in that other America.

UNDER OBSERVATION

We, in North America, are proud of our freedom to move about freely at anytime without restriction,

Upon moving to that other America I soon discovered that the authorities there at least seemed to be more vigilant. In Argentina, we all had to spend some time in the police station downtown to get our official "cedulas" or identification cards The inconvenience came from having to spend so many hours in different unending lines to get fingerprinted, photographed, etc. We were to carry our Cedula at all times. It had to be kept updated and in order. We soon learned that as foreigners, in particular, we were observed and the authorities knew who and where we were, and what we were doing.

I admit I didn't particularly enjoy having officials whom I suppose were from the Argentine FBI or immigration office visit my office once a year to check if I was still living at José C Paz 1020 in Acassuso, if I still had three children and still worked at the same place. A bit more red tape was required which some might call a denial of freedom. However, I didn't feel it to be all that objectionable. As long as I stayed out of trouble I found no room to complain. Although I had to carry the identification, it was seldom checked.

Bolivia also required permits in addition to local passports to travel within the country. One had to secure a certificate of good conduct from the police as well as a certificate of good health from an approved medical doctor. When I went to Chile in 1946 to get out of the altitude for a time, it was necessary to get a certificate of good health first, in spite of the fact that I was going to Chile primarily for health reasons. Needless to say, the doctor gave me the document, since there is always a fee involved.

I discovered that with a little bit of "coima" or gratuity, the rough edges could be smoothed a little. It just seemed to be a part of the game of getting along. One did not have to wait quite as long. Things could be done today instead of "mañana."

A friend asked me to accompany him as he visited a prison in Mendoza. I had no fear of the convicts, although they told me that they were murderers, thieves etc. They seemed almost eager to talk to me. Actually the tension I felt was from the fact that I had to leave all my precious documents with the officer at the entrance desk of the prison. There I was inside a jail, totally bare of all of my precious documents, my I.D., my wallet, etc. I felt rather helpless, and realized how a loss of freedom must affect the incarcerated. As I left I offered a personal prayer for the prisoners and another of gratitude to be outside in the fresh air again with all my documents.

I do get disturbed, at times, when I read of the ease with which members of the criminal element here in the U.S. come to and go from the U.S with what appears to be little restriction or when I read about the large number of people who are at large in the U.S. illegally, having overstayed their tourist visas or with illegal or forged documentation. They have enjoyed as well as abused the freedoms in our country with no sense of responsibility for the rights and privileges they enjoy. When later they are possibly apprehended they even threaten to destroy those freedoms and values. The falsification of documents and other similar forgeries could in time destroy those rights which we confess to cherish. Total freedom can lead to anarchy.

I hope that I am a peace loving and law abiding citizen and feel that other residents of the country should be the same, respecting the law of the land.

Many agree that our criminal justice system could be improved, but real improvement has to come from within as one learns to appreciate and respect the values we enjoy. That holds true for both the Americas.

PUBLIC SAFETY

For twenty years (1947-1967) we relied almost exclusively on public transportation, especially in the cities of Lima and Buenos Aires. At no time did we feel threatened or insecure. It was a two hour trip on three different bus lines from our house in the suburbs to Ward College in Ramos Mejía. One could make this trip at almost any hour of the day or night. Or one could take the train to Retiro, the central station and not feel that it might be dangerous to walk through the station. We did not read or hear of any shootings or other incidents. The only discomfort came from overcrowding. The busses and subways were always crowded, or so it seemed. A woman might feel a roaming hand trying to make a pass, but would know of no violence. The same was true of the city of Lima on the busses and streetcars.

There were pickpockets on crowded vehicles. We had to take precautions, especially at holiday times. I carried my wallet inside my jacket pocket. One colleague was a tall 6 feet 6 inches. Occasionally he would find the hand of a much shorter person trying to reach up to his pocket. Since he was so much taller, he was able to remove the hand of the intruder before the latter had a chance to remove the wallet.

Just before Christmas, another colleague took his small son to town to do some shopping. On the crowded bus, he placed the boy on his shoulders. After selecting an item they wished to purchase he reached for his wallet only to find that it was missing. He brought the boy back home, got some more money and went back to complete the transaction. A couple of hours after he had returned home, a little girl came to the door saying she had found the wallet on the street. (Perhaps she hoped for a reward.) Of course, it had been neatly cleared of the money it had contained.

That same evening this same friend took the bus to Callao to attend the closing ceremonies at that school. He was carrying another wallet, but it also was taken. After that he vowed he would only carry a New Testament in his pocket and strangely enough, had no further experience with pickpockets! The main problem was not the loss of money but rather the problem of identification cards and the time and inconvenience of having to secure new I.D.

One rather unusual and annoying incident occurred on the suburban train to Acassuso. An Argentine gentleman had fallen asleep on his way home from work. His mouth was open. A North American student on his way home, and smoking a cigarette, saw this as an excellent opportunity to show off his maturity and superiority. He flicked the ashes into the open mouth of the Argentine gent who awoke and shouted, but there was no violence. The North American youth proudly marched down the aisle in triumph, having found such a convenient ashtray. I think that I was more ashamed and outraged by the conduct of the student posing as the triumphant and superior American than was the Argentine gentleman who did not make an issue over the incident.

There were occasional traffic accidents by busses or even by train, but we noted no purposeful danger caused by misconduct. In fact, it was surprising that there were not more traffic accidents since many drivers followed the law of the jungle.

Years ago Mr. Roy Rubottom, who was President Eisenhower's representative in South America and one time ambassador to Argentina said that one afternoon he tried to drive around the city as a courteous gentleman. He claimed that after an hour he gave up. That was hyperbole, but one could understand his dilemma.

The traffic in the cities of Brazil moves at a rapid pace. The story is told that when two bus drivers in Rio de Janeiro met after a day's work, one would ask the other, "¿Cuántos comiste hoy?' (How many people or cars did you hit today?) I was told that if the driver fled the accident and wasn't caught within ten days, he could not be charged. Maybe it was like the old "cities of refuge" as described in the Old Testament.

Although one seldom heard of burglaries in Argentina, the neighborhood would agree to hire a "sereno" or watchman to patrol the streets at night. He would ride around on his bicycle and to assure us that he was on the job he would blow his little whistle from time to time to let us know that he was in the neighborhood. It was comforting to hear his whistle during the night hours whenever one awakened. We felt safe and secure.

LET'S EAT!

When it comes to the matter of nourishment, it is not only a question of when do we eat but also "What do we eat?

In Chile one had a tea rather than a coffee break in late morning. It was called "te once" (11 o'clock). However, tea in the afternoon was called "Te" and served late in the afternoon was "Te Cena" (supper), followed by the main meal which was never served before 8:00 p.m.

When we arrived in Bolivia we were offered a snack which was called a "salteña" (a kind of a meat pie, very peppery or "picante" served with a soft drink called Inca Cola. Meals all started with "caldo" (broth or soup). I preferred "minestrone". Most of the vegetables were for decoration, and rice and or potatoes were the basics. Occasionally we had beef, but it was usually too tough to eat. I would chew for a while and then give up. I was never sure if the poor cattle had such a tough time grazing on those Andean mountain sides or if it was just too difficult to get the temperature to a tenderizing level. Water, for example, doesn't boil at 212 degrees in the altitude. It boiled at about 180. I would boil water for shaving, and then, while the water was still bubbling, put my finger into the water with no damage done.

One of the specialties in the meat line and quite edible was "lengua picante" (spiced tongue). It was very hot but tender enough, the only piece of meat that was. I don't know which variety of pepper was used, but it seemed to be a stronger variety of jalapeno and was called "ají."

When I had a meal at which even the local people were eating with tears in their eyes, I knew that the pepper would burn from my lips to my stomach. After a time one would become accustomed to the "heat" and after that one would think that most food lacked "seasoning".

Another favorite in the Andes was the "cui - ses" (guinea pigs). Not much meat, but the gravy helped to give the illusion of real meat when served with rice. The "cuises" tasted a little like squirrel, but were of lighter color and texture. Once after I had returned to the U.S I was visiting some friends and made the mistake of telling some children that I used to eat the guinea pigs. The children were shocked that I could eat their pets and I realized that I had "put my foot in my mouth."

Another common and popular food, often served as stew, was based on "mondongo" (stomach) and tripe. However, I admit that these were not among my favorites.

We were served a lot of corn, from "humita," a kind of corn mush, to the several varieties and colors of corn itself, even a purple one, which was used in making "chicha morada", a type of punch, made by boiling pineapple and the purple corn together. Then pieces of chopped apple or quince would be floated on top. The corn dishes were good, or as they said "rico". If the food was very good, one would say "riquísimo." When one sat at the table usually the host would say "buen provecho." This meant, “May the meal be of value to you. Enjoy!"

For us the expert for the local cuisine was Sra. Pacheco. She knew what to fix and how to fix it. She prepared all the special meals and her meals were always "riquísimo". She prepared meals for the summer camp. This was a long laborious project and thinking to help her I bought a large pressure cooker so that the cooking time would be lessened. But the good Señora would not use this labor saving device. Her response was that she really liked to cook, and she liked to spend the longer time doing the thing she liked to do. She did not want more "time" for other things.

I really enjoyed a dish called "Papas a la Huancaina" (Potatoes Huancayan style.) They were potatoes which had been boiled, mashed and doctored up with "picante" and other condiments. They were "hot", spicy and delicious.

I learned to like “chuño,” too. They were the Bolivian method of freeze dried potatoes. The barefooted Indians would trample these small potatoes, and then they were dried in the sun and frozen on the mountainside. It was something like a rather gray and possibly dirty hominy with a similar texture, and was served fried with eggs.

Another favorite was "arroz con pollo" (rice with chicken). Although the Irish potato was native to the area, most people ate as much if not more rice than potatoes. In fact, it was not uncommon to have rice three times a day.

We were given a grain which I hadn't eaten before. It was said to be very nutritious, easy to grow and a real boon to agriculture in the region. It was something like barley and was very good in soup ("quinua").

I have not mentioned the great beef (steaks and asados) of the River Plate. Workmen and laborers would build their fire and "roast" their piece of beef for their noon meal. A steak was served "medio caballo" with one fried egg on top or "a caballo" with two.

I must mention a banquet honoring a member of the staff. It was held at the finest hotel in the city. It was so special that they even served "squab.". I can still remember Srta. Adela. She anchored the bird on her plate with her fork, and then she gingerly took her knife and tried to cut off a bit of meat. The squab was served with the "head" still intact (so one could be sure what one was eating). Every time she would start to slice, the head of the bird would move from side to side as if to say "No, no." After several attempts she put her knife down and said "No way. Even the bird is telling me to stop."

Peru was great for fish and for a while we even had "whale meat" steaks.

When I visited the Chanchamayo area which was a jungle or semi-jungle area, I was introduced to some other delicacies. One was monkey meat. It reminded me a little of rabbit. I was not excited about it, and I would not want to have it on a regular diet.

There was quite a difference between the diets of the high sierra and the lower jungle area. One of our visitors returned from a five-day trip and said he had not been able to identify positively any of the food eaten during that time. "Heart of the palm" was fixed as a salad and that was quite acceptable.

It was impossible to plan a menu which would satisfy those who had come from Bolivia, Chile, Peru, Argentina and the U.S. Bolivians could not eat a salad made of carrots, cabbage, and apples, because one could not eat fruit and vegetables in the same dish. Lorla once asked the cooks to prepare a "tuna" salad and was surprised to find that a salad had been prepared from the fruit of the cactus called "tuna." It was different.

I once suggested that for an early morning breakfast we might have orange juice, sweet rolls and coffee. Their response was, "But Señor, it is not a picnic." They wanted hot tamales and hot chocolate. Try it sometime after your Easter sunrise service.

We introduced apple pie which they seemed to enjoy. They called it "apple pie de manzana". “Manzana” is an apple so what else would it be. However, they soon had “apple pie de chocolate,” “apple pie de limon,” etc.

The people were not as strict or finicky on matters of sanitation but they were artists in their own way. I recall a young lady in the diner of the International train. Desserts aren't usually that special, often just fruit. A young lady had been served a large delicious apple on her plate. I watched almost entranced by her artistry. She never touched the apple with her hands but with a knife and fork she pared and sculptured that apple so skillfully. All she had left was a bit of the core and the seeds.

One soon notices that in that other America many people use the European method of using the fork in the left hand where it is kept while cutting with the knife in the right-hand. I think it was Dwight Eisenhower who used this European custom and preferred it and spoke of its convenience, rather than to have to shift the knife and fork from time to time while eating. If the food is good, I can enjoy eating either way in both Americas.

¡BUEN PROVECHO!

COFFEE BREAK?

One usually thinks of a cafeteria as a place where one selects from a wide variety of food in a kind of self-serve arrangement and then sits down and eats without the attention of waiter or waitress or "server" as they are called today. The word itself actually goes back to an old Spanish custom. A "cafetería" is actually a coffee shop where one goes to have a drink of coffee. These "cafeterías" are very popular places. One can go up to a café (coffee bar) and have a demitasse of coffee or sit down with friends and spend an hour or two in friendly conversation, or talk business. Major business transactions can take place over a cup or cups of coffee, so it can be a social or business occasion. I once made a sale of 50,000 Bibles over coffee in a "cafetería" in Buenos Aires.

In the early morning it is usually a cup of coffee with milk ("café con leche" or "café au lait.") Then for the rest of the day it is usually a "cafecito" or "cafezinño" in Brazil) which means a demitasse, usually half filled with sugar, then the thick, black coffee syrup is poured to fill the cup and swallowed with a gulp or possibly two. In some places water is dripped over a large amount of coffee to effect a very thick and black syrup and sold in bottles. It is "essence" and one can add very hot water to get the preferred thickness. As a rule our Latin friends prefer a much stronger concoction of coffee than we do. On one occasion Dr. Jorge P. Howard was a guest in Peru. My wife served an ordinary cup of American style coffee. He asked,

"Do you call this coffee?" She then took some of the pure essence of coffee, and without dilution, added three or four teaspoons of our instant powdered coffee. It was almost too thick to stir. He then took a swallow and remarked: "Well, that's more like it." Some Argentine friends said U.S. coffee tasted like some dirty socks had been boiled in water, and were amazed that we dared to call that coffee.

On our first trip south we flew from New Orleans to Mérida, Mexico. We arrived there about 2:00 a.m. I asked for a cup of coffee and was served some of that black syrup. It awakened me with a start. It seemed so bitter. As I visited the Syrio-Lebanese men in their shops in Tucumán one morning, each offered me a demitasse of the essence. After a few visits I began to feel "high".

My recollection of excellent coffee was on a Pullman car traveling from Nashville to Buffalo, New York. It was called "dining car" coffee and it was perfect for my taste.

"BEBIDAS"

In Argentina one finds "maté," a Brazilian holly, or sometimes called Paraguayan tea infused in a decorated gourd, and sipped through a "bombilla," or metal straw. This is imbibed throughout the day, and people, especially men, walk around on the streets, carrying their maté with them and sipping as they conduct their business.

Of course our soft drinks are quite well known. "Siete oop" (7•Up®) is popular and Mr. "Bud" Farnsworth, manager of Coca Cola® in Buenos Aires in the sixties, said that more Coca Cola was sold in the River Plate area than in New York City and Westchester County combined. Someone has remarked that we are responsible for the "Coca Cola colonization" of the world.

As for their wines, Mendocino wines of Argentina are reasonably priced and good and those in Chile are relatively well known as well.

POP THE CORN AND CRACK THE COCAINE

Our technical expertise is often evident in South America. The Incan civilization on the west side of South America made use of and developed many vegetable and garden products. Some of these vegetables still are unknown in the United States. Potatoes were native to the area as was corn or maize in its several varieties and colors.

When we first went to Peru in 1946 there was no popcorn to be found. On our return from furlough in 1951 we made certain that we packed several pounds (which, incidentally, broke from its container and circulated among the other items in the trunk.) We were back in the city of Lima a few days when we discovered popcorn machines installed on many street corners! They had developed the product. We had to teach them how to produce it in the form of popped corn. It was a product of our ingenuity, a triumph of our salesmanship to sell popcorn to the Peruvians.

Some of our technical improvements are not always beneficial to mankind. One example of our technical know-how to improve humanity was to take the simple coca leaves which can be bought at almost any market place in Bolivia and in other countries as well, and with technological skill produce what is called "crack cocaine" which gave the lowly coca leaf a potency it had not achieved before. With tongue in cheek one can again say that our brilliance sometimes exceeds our common sense for although it creates a financial bonanza, it also creates problems in drug addiction which are difficult to curb or solve.

A CLEARING MIST

The Humboldt current brings a shroud of mist or fog over the city of Lima during the so-called winter months (May-October). It is called "Garúa." Since the sun literally doesn't shine all winter long, one gets the impression of living in a damp basement. One kept a light burning in the closet to prevent mold forming on one's shoes, or clothes. There was no central heating. We wore two or three sweaters. It never actually rained, but at times one wished it would to clear the atmosphere.

One day we did have a small shower of rain. The local people seemed to think that the end of the world had come. The people ran to the church to seek shelter, not so much from the moisture, but to be in a "safe place". They had not seen a shower of rain. It lasted only a few minutes and when it was finished a friend and I went out to play tennis on a clay court. One could truthfully say that it still had not ever really rained in Lima. Moisture from the Pacific Ocean lifts over the Andes and deposits abundant rainfall in the Amazon basin on the other side of the mountains.

A disease endemic in Peru in the fifties, especially during those cold, humid months of fog and mist, was tuberculosis. Many friends would simply report that they had received their death sentence upon learning that they had tuberculosis. Many of the poor would come out of the countryside to try to find a better life in the city. They would move into a poor hovel made of cardboard boxes, in the "barriadas" or slums, very possibly where the previous residents had succumbed to tuberculosis. Dr. Jorge Sarmiento, a Peruvian, said it was a vicious cycle which was repeated over and over again. Thus the mist which hung over Lima and the coast was more than a simple "garúa."

Like coming out of the mist my knowledge of the Spanish language had improved to the point that my staff claimed that they could no longer notice that I was a gringo. I had to take part in the Peruvian national parade on July 28 and had the honor of sitting with the dignitaries at the program since two of our teachers were to be awarded medals of honor by the national government for their outstanding service to education in Peru.

Occasionally we had visits from teachers from the U.S either on a sabbatical holiday or retired, who upon seeing the need, would volunteer to teach simply for room and board. That was pleasing since someone else had appreciated what was being done. One of those teachers was Elizabeth Davis from Jackson, Missouri and another was Ruth Tiffany from Chevy Chase, Maryland.

"¡SALUD!"

A common concern in every culture is the matter of health. The "witch doctor" or "curandero" may be found in many parts of that other America. The "curandero" is not exactly what one might call a "witch doctor". There are probably more "curanderos" (healers) who try to practice healing without a license. Governments usually try to control them especially if they are practicing their methods with the desire to have financial gain. Some rare or unusual approaches to medicine or healing are practiced. Pharmaceutical companies still search these regions for plants and herbs which may provide a cure for some of the ailments which afflict people in our times.

One should mention the early medicine and surgery practiced in the time of the Incas in Peru. One can visit museums there and see the metal tools used by those early healers in their operations. They used those rather primitive instruments to perform brain surgery to help a wounded soldier to recover from an open wound in the head. While we were there in the early fifties a Dr. Graña Garland used some of those early Inca instruments to perform a trepanation as proof that it had been done and could still be done. The desire to prolong life and health is a procedure of long standing. During Inca times bodies were wrapped in gunny bags in a fetal position, and in the arid areas seem to have been pretty well preserved. As a person walks through these museums and sees these "momias" with their corresponding numbers one wonders if the same might be done with members of our so-called civilization. It appears that there has always been an appreciation of life and of staying alive.

One can take note also that an Argentinean, Bernardo A. Houssay, was a Nobel prize winner in medicine in 1947 for his study of the pituitary.

Some doctors were homeopaths, who seemed to recommend taking small doses of medicine which came in small bottles. The medicine would produce symptoms similar to the disease being treated. I sometimes felt like I was substituting one pain for another, like having a headache instead of a backache. I think that most doctors in North America are allopaths, offering treatments opposite in nature to the disease in order to eliminate the pain or problem .

I was surprised by the absence of chiropractors and, on the other hand, the abundance of faith healers. A business man in Ushuaia introduced me to his small son who seemed to be quite healthy. He told me how ill the lad had been until their maid suggested he give a faith healer a chance to pray with them for the restoration of the boy's health. He knew about mind over matter and still was amazed at the complete return to normalcy and almost incredulous that he did not even have to visit a pharmacy to buy medicine. He had become a firm believer in faith healing.

I had a good Algerian friend who owned the French gymnasium about two blocks from our house in Acassuso. There I was doing exercises and getting massages before they became the "in" thing here in the U.S. At a time of tension or strain, it was good to get a massage for relief and relaxation. Furthermore, his wife was a "pedicuro". She would take care of one's feet and nails just as a manicurist does in the U.S., the difference was that the charge was so minimal that one felt guilty if one didn't use their services. I suppose there were hundreds of unlicensed "pedicuros" in Argentina who did the work of a podiatrist. The services were well received and I admit that I miss the convenience and inexpensive treatment I received from my Algerian friends nearby.

Whether here or there we look to our health.

EMERGENCY 911

In many areas of the U.S, medical service is very much at a premium. In that other America it is even more apparent especially in the rural areas. Requirements for medical school and the M.D. degree are not as stringent there. A youth wanting to become a "médico" had an easier time in that he only needed to finish secondary or high school before going directly into medical school. No bachelors degree or attendance for four years at an university was required. He had gained four years on his or her North American counterpart.

Some of these young people enter in to practice briefly and then make application for study in the U.S to specialize in their field of interest. There are dozens of towns and communities here in the U.S. which are clamoring for a medical doctor to serve their needs. Since it is an emergency situation, and there is a shortage of medical doctors, these young people from that other America are welcomed to serve as full time "médicos" after a year or two of study in the U.S. Some have limited experience or preparation. That is not to say that all these youths are not able and responsible and many are or will become excellent physicians and surgeons. Even serving as a medical doctor in a small rural community, these young people will be earning much more income than if they had stayed in their own country where, perhaps, they would have more prestige but less income and conveniences. Once he gets to North America and begins to specialize in his field, he has less desire to return to be of service to his countrymen. Here he has excellent equipment available and is offered the service of a community hospital. He or she has found a quick road to success.

Some North American youth find it very difficult to get into medical school because of the requirements and because there are more applications than vacancies. Some have become aware of the technique of getting a degree in that other America and then follow the example of specialized study in the U.S. in internal medicine, gynecology or almost any other field of interest in our prestigious medical schools.

I have recommended several young people, who aspired to become physicians, to come to the U.S. for training. I always tried to get them to give a good account of themselves in their profession wherever they might be. I admit that I have made some mistakes. Just because a person seems bright and has shown fairly good credentials does not mean that he will be a credit to the profession. Some of the brightest and sharpest may turn out to be clever devils. Then again one may be just half right.

A colleague had two sons who studied medicine. One attained his M.D. in Peru after high school, and secured entrance to study in his field of specialization at one of the U.S. medical schools, worked for a time in the U.S.and then returned to Peru. His brother finished his M.D. work in his native country. He did not go to the U.S. for further training. They worked together for a while. They were quite professional and were doing well. They decided to open a clinic to serve the underprivileged in their community. It seemed like a very high ideal of service. One day the local authorities placed a sign over their clinic door and boarded it up. One had begun using his knowledge and connections to deal in drugs illegally. I can still see that father trudging slowly down the street to visit his son in prison.

COMING APART AT THE SEAMS

Through the years I was required to have three hernia repairs of the inguinal type, two on the right side, and one on the left. To keep them international, I had the first in Chicago in 1940 and was required to stay hospitalized for two weeks. A general anesthetic was used. The second was for the left side and was done in Lima, Peru, in the 1950s, also done under general anesthesia. Although I was told to remain in bed for a week, for some reason, I awoke in the middle of the first night, and found myself walking around in the room. The third was done in Buenos Aires, Argentina. The right side had given way and required another repair. Science had advanced, and local anesthesia was used. The hospital stay was briefer. I got along pretty well and on my first night at home helped to capture a bat which had come in while the door was open.

In order to hold me together for a while, I recall that I was wrapped tightly with a "faja", which is a Spanish word meaning “girdle.” One of our young daughters asked me why I was wearing a girdle. One of the other girls said, "That is more like a "Brazil." The first retorted, "No, that goes higher up."

A few days ago I ate at a local fast food store. I saw "fajitas" on the menu and I asked the young lady if she knew what a "fajita" was. She said, "It is like a little meat pie." She asked if I wanted beef or chicken . Then I asked the young girl, "Do you know what that word means in Spanish? You have probably never worn one but it means a little girdle." I think she thought that was enough Spanish lesson for the day and I enjoyed my chicken "fajita."

"FARMACIAS"

It was much less of a hassle to buy the medicine one needed or at least thought one wanted. One didn't even have to know how to spell it, but if one could come close to pronouncing it, one could buy it. Prescriptions were not required for many items. Medications with sulpha or penicillin could be purchased over the counter as could many other items in the several countries in which we lived in that other America. A physician recommended that I take Terramycin once a year to avoid problems with amoebic dysentery. I did this for years.

In other words, the rules for buying medicines were not very strict. The attitude was more casual. Of course, one ran the risk of taking the wrong medicine, but there were always friendly pharmacists who would give guidelines. This was a boon for many patients who had neither the time or money to see a doctor. On the other hand, the drugstores were there to dispense the drugs but did not carry other miscellaneous items and were not mini-markets or variety stores.

On our arrival in Lima fifty years ago, we were surprised to find big yellow signs in the shape of a tube of toothpaste advertising Kolynos in green letters. It was a brand which was not well known to us. These signs were displayed over the streetlights along the main avenues at frequent intervals. We thought it was an unique way of promoting good dental care.

Now that I am back in the U.S. I fear that I have been victimized by the constant bombardment of advertisements of over the counter remedies which will cure any and every thing. Our pharmacies are full of these items, with many brands competing against one another.

I have a friend who at 103 still goes to his office fairly regularly. He still enjoys good health. It must be in his genes and not in his jeans, which may have some patent medicine in their pockets, but I doubt it. In both Americas, our goal is still "Stay healthy."

"HACIENDO COLAS"

As a rule our South American friends were known for their individualism. But they did conform to custom when they saw it as advantageous. I recall the crowds trying to get a "tranvía" (streetcar) from the stop near the Hotel Bolívar in Lima in order to go to Callao. They actually made long lines and patiently awaited their turn before trying to board. They were usually quite orderly. However, an occasional youth would climb atop the car in order to get a free ride for the nine or ten kilometers. Perhaps he found it more comfortable than trying to hold on to the door while barely having a foot on the step along with many others in the same position.

An unusual sight was in Asunción, Paraguay where in the late fifties, a special kind of "tranvía" was built with a large lift up type of door in the rear. Its route was to the cemetery. The mourners would form a cola to board the street car via the unusual door followed by the coffin which was shoved in after them. At little expense the funeral procession made its way to the cemetery for the interment.

"Colas" were a way of life.

UPSIDE DOWN WEATHER

It always seemed so strange to have such hot weather at Christmas. We even went to the trouble of bringing in some evergreen branches for Christmas, decorating them with ornaments, when really the beautiful flowers of spring and summer were so much more in order. One had to go South and not North to find cooler weather. It did seem strange to see store windows decorated with cotton snow. One felt that "Papa Noel," the usual name for Santa Claus, should wear lighter weight clothes to endure the heat, perhaps even a swim suit because the beach season was officially blessed and opened on December 8.

My colleague in Argentina, Sr. David O. Somoza, and I went one year to Tierra del Fuego at or during the Christmas season. It was very hot in Buenos Aires. The weather was very pleasant all the way down to Ushuaia. Many Chileans will say that Punta Arenas (Sand Point) is the southernmost city of the Americas. The Argentines will claim that Ushuaia has that distinction. My opinion is that even though Punta Arenas may be a bit larger, the rapidly growing area of Ushuaia is a bit farther South and East. Ushuaia is a free port so many items can be brought in duty free. One is surprised by the number of foreigners living at the bottom of that other America. There has been quite an influx of Japanese business men. I was told that much of the limited amount of coal found in Argentina was mined by Chilean residents.

Since the seasons are reversed one could enjoy the weather in what one here usually thinks of as the worst heat of the summer. There was a beautiful tourist hotel in Ushuaia. As I recall it bore the name "Albatross" for what reason I do not know. The food and the accommodations were superb, and one had a wonderful view of the Beagle Channel through the picture windows. I was struck by the weird appearance of the atmosphere as one looked out across the South Atlantic towards the land of Antartica. There seemed to be a kind of haze as over another world.

I had a good visit with an Argentine business man whose store looked out on the Beagle Channel. I asked him about the winter (July-August) weather there. He said that the snow would be over a meter deep just outside the front door of his store. The east coast of Argentina has a very nice climate, but the deep south evidently had weather comparable with Minnesota. Since the seasons are reversed, a common statement in Argentina was that if a person made it through the month of August which is usually wet and damp, he would probably live or survive for another year.

Much of the area of Southern Argentina is thinly populated, but one will find large “estancias” or ranches with thousands of sheep. Early settlers from Scotland still own many of these extensive land holdings where there are more sheep than people. The fine wool is known and shipped around the world.

In Buenos Aires I met the owner of a Scandinavian travel agency who made arrangements for the first organized tour to Antartica. He had even made arrangements with the Argentine navy to clear a path through the ice floes. One of the trips ended in near disaster, but the group was rescued and brought back to safety. Travel agencies now arrange such trips quite frequently during the Argentine summer months (Dec.-Feb.)

To get a bit of the history of the area I recommend a book entitled, "The Uttermost part of the Earth" by E. Lucas Bridges. There were settlers there even before Argentina itself became a country. One can also read of Darwin's early venture to that part of the world.

"EL NIÑO"

An important factor affecting both Americas is "El Nino." When the current coming out of the South Pacific hits the western shores of South America the resulting weather pattern is known as "El Niño". Since its effect is usually felt around Christmas time and following, I assume that it gets its identification from the Christ Child. Meteorologists have been studying "El Niño" for years but it is rather erratic and unpredictable, especially when California is hit by heavy rains and flooding, and Peru may miss much of its usual cool, cloudy winter.

Just as "El Niño" is not always predictable, so it is with relations between the Americas. "El Niño" at times deviates from its normal course and can have unusual consequences. The normal relationships between the nations of the Americas may also find stormy weather. It may be the development of economic and trade relations between the countries, or a stir over illegal aliens. Meanwhile studies of "El Niño" and the relations between the Americas requires constant vigilance and evaluation.

TURN ON THE LIGHTS

When we first went to Bolivia in 1945 we learned that most electric power was supposedly 220 volts as in much of the rest of South America. However, we discovered that the actual available power supply from the power company seldom reached the 220 volts. In fact it was usually between 180 to 210 volts. We had to get some step-up transformers to augment the power supply. We called them "boosters". Since most of the appliances we had brought with us were designed for 110 volt, 60 cycle current, we first had to use the transformers to bring the voltage down to what was approximately 110 volts to allow us to use our appliances with a relative degree of safety. One problem was that the boosters also consumed current, and as more and more boosters were used the amount of power available was actually reduced. It reminds me of two medications I am taking at present, one is to raise my blood pressure and the other is to lower it. One trick I used temporarily to increase the brightness of the light in the house was to insert a 110 volt bulb in our lights during the early evening hours when power was being consumed in greater quantities, but about 9 p.m. when people began to turn off their lights and the availability of power increased I had to be sure to remove the bulb or suddenly notice that the 110 volt bulb had blown. It was great while it lasted.

Then we moved to Lima, Peru in November, 1946 where water was scarce but electric power was plentiful. Although the Rimac river did not supply enough water for the city, hydroelectric power which came from water channeled down from some of the Andean mountain streams, provided excellent lighting for the city. In fact, it was so bright that when driving one's car at night one was required to use only the parking lights. There were warning signs along the roads which read “No encandile” which meant "Don't flash on your headlights" since it might blind the driver of an approaching car.

However, there was a shortage of potable water in the city of Lima. Our gardener would do his work after midnight when there was sufficient water available to water the lawn. We had to place large tanks on the roof to collect water at night when the pressure was high enough to push the water to that level, and then hope that enough water had filled the tanks to meet the needs during the day. The time came when that supply did not meet the demand and faucets would be left open, only to cause difficulties when the water would have enough pressure again. We came home one evening to find water running down the stairs. I purchased a rural type electric pump and pressure tank to supply us with water for the 24 hours of the day.

One was never totally sure of the quality or the purity of the water supply in Lima. We drank boiled water during the ten years we lived there. The water was boiled and stored in a tall crock with a faucet at the bottom. It seemed a little flat at first, but one soon became accustomed to it. We were not consistent since we drank only boiled water, but we still brushed our teeth with tap water without giving it much thought. Still when we read of more recent outbreaks of cholera and dysentery in Peru, we feel that perhaps we were just fortunate. Possibly some guardian angel was keeping our water clean for us.

In Buenos Aires, on the other hand, in the late 1950s, there was an ample water supply, but we were at times without electric power. Power outages were called "apagones" and we were usually warned in advance of the days or nights when our sector of the city would be without electricity. After months of these "apagones" I finally broke down and bought an Alladin type lamp. From then on there were no more of the stoppages! One adapted to the inconvenience, but it seemed strange that a city of 10 million people would suffer that inconvenience. Perhaps that was part of the problem, too little electric power for that many people.

When the power was off, the television service was also off. Thus one could not even watch the re-runs of U.S. programs with Spanish subtitles. We couldn't hear Tato Bores, a political satirist, who with his humor, got away with a lot more than we expected until he evidently did go a bit too far and was no longer on the air. The stars, such as Pinky, presenting the commercials, were well or better known than the stars of the regular programs. There was no regard for time, commercials were not made to fit a certain time slot. As a result scheduled programs would be as much as 15-30 minutes late as the day lengthened.

A TIDAL WAVE?

One evening we received a report that a "marejada" or "marmoto" (sea quake) as it was called in Peru, had occurred somewhere in the Pacific. Residents in the port city of Callao became quite alarmed. In fact they became so worried that the "tidal wave" would hit their shore that hundreds started walking to higher ground in Lima. Some of our colleagues who lived and worked in Callao were concerned and asked what I was going to do about it. I was born a Missourian and I "had to be shown." I really didn't believe that we were in any danger. I could imagine that multitude of people slowly trudging along the nine kilometer stretch from Callao to Lima caught up in the traffic jam of the busses and "colectivos" (cars that carried many passengers along a certain route for hire.) After all, the report had said that the "Tsunami" (tidal wave) had occurred across the Pacific Ocean. I could not see how that could cause any danger so quickly to us so far away. We heard that some started prayer vigils. I decided to go to bed and sleep through whatever was supposedly about to happen.

A matter of graver concern were the "temblores" or earthquakes and tremors. The lighter shakes were the "temblores" and the heavier and more destructive ones were generally known as "terremotos," although I understand that the shallower ones can be more destructive. There had been a major earthquake sometime before our arrival in Peru in 1946 and the coast was littered with large blocks of cement from fallen buildings. The neighborhood dogs would begin to howl, since they seemed to sense, feel or hear the danger before humans could. One could usually hear a rumbling coming from deep down in the earth before the actual shake began. The local people must have slept with one foot out of the bed, and our neighbors would be out in the streets before I would realize what was happening. If a "temblor" occurred at night one became paralyzed with fear and it was hard to decide whether to go out and join them or better to stay in bed. If a "temblor" occurred in the day time I feared mainly for our hundreds of students since I knew that our buildings certainly were not earthquake proof.

One quite strong “temblor” was centered around Cuzco on Memorial Day. It caused a near panic when the adobe tombs began to crumble and coffins and bodies came tumbling out into view. The visitors in the cemeteries fled in terror. Many thought the end of time had come.

These “temblores” were daily occurrences. Still, one never really got used to them and one's heart seemed to stand still as one waited to see how strong it was going to be. They would be over by the time we would decide to stand in the doorway or seek shelter. Fortunately, we had no serious earthquake in the decade we were in Peru and the threatened wall of water which had been predicted did not arrive.

THE ALTITUDE AND OXYGEN

The only thing which I could enjoy in the altitude was the view. One was impressed and almost overwhelmed by the magnitude and magnificence of mountains—like Illimani which towered high above the city of La Paz. I had read in Time magazine of a place described as "mountain top" La Paz, only to discover that despite its elevation of 12,000 feet it was actually nestled in a kind of valley which seemed to sink out of the Altiplano which was another 1000 feet higher. The airport in La Paz is one of the highest commercial airports in the world. It seemed to take forever for the plane to become airborne at that altitude.

I didn't get along very well with the altitude. On one occasion I did try to accompany some of the students on a climb of Mount Tunari, at the edge of the Cochabamba valley, which was at an elevation of 8,500 feet. Mount Tunari was only about 17,400 feet high but after scaling a little over 15,000 feet, I turned around and headed for lower ground. Some of the students didn't make it either, so I didn't feel too guilty.

I felt tension and pressure at the altitude in Cochabamba, and couldn't sleep well at night. I began to lose so much weight that our medical doctor suggested a month out of the altitude in Antofagasta, Chile at sea level. First, I had to get a certificate of good health from local "médicos" to allow me to travel. It was a formidable trip. One had to take the train to Oruro which was west and south and at an altitude of approximately 13,500 feet and then on to the town of Uyuni and across to the Atacama desert (said to be the driest in the world), passing by one of the highest copper mines in the world and down through the nitrate area to the coastal city of Antofagasta, Chile, seemingly placed at the water's edge at the bottom of the Andean slope. The Maury hotel was built at the ocean edge. Part of the building was on stilts just over the water. Some friends visited us. The beating of the waves under the building was so strong that one of our visitors asked to leave because she began to feel sea sick from the noise and vibration of the building. In order to keep warm in our hotel room, we would fill the bathtub with hot water and let that warmth penetrate the air. After several hours we would do a repeat performance.

A naval officer had lunch with us and invited me to go out on the rocky beach to catch a "pulpo" (octopus). The naval officer showed me how to get beside one of the sleeping "pulpos," rub its back to make it loosen its grip on the rock and then capture it. We then took it to the chef who was asked to prepare it for our evening meal. It was prepared in a tomato sauce and served over rice. My opinion was that it offered a very chewy but not too delectable entree. Try it, you may like it. I don't plan a repeat.

INSECTS

One finds insects in both Americas, but the one which left the greatest impression on me in that other America was the lowly flea. My first experience with an invasion of them was in Bolivia. They seemed to find me and delight in making life a bit miserable for me. They were so attracted to me that when I saw a dog, I began to scratch. If I went to the theater they would be there waiting for me in the seats or wherever. I knew that they were prevalent in both Americas, but as a gringo I was seemingly chosen as a prize attraction. They seemed to hide in the cracks between the tiles of a floor. I never had to find them. They always found me. I thought that perhaps we had reached a truce, since they didn't seem to bother me so much after a year. Then we moved to Peru in 1946.

Possibly it was a new breed, but the fleas began to attack me voraciously there also. I was a selected target, but some people seemed to be immune. A trip to the post office or a bank would mean they had found me. We had one upholstered chair in the living room which was especially infested with "pulgas." When visitors came our small children would warn them not to sit in that flea chair. One time when I itched all over I had my wife count the number of bites. There were seventy-seven. No wonder they made me feel miserable.

In jest it is said that the mosquito is the

Minnesota state bird. That state does not have a monopoly. They are in that other America as well. I read an article in the National Geographic in which the author claimed that a person who survived five years of mosquitoes in Brazil, would either find the mosquito less annoying or would have succumbed to malaria or yellow fever. We sent 40-50 young people on a summer camp project in the jungle area of Peru. It was unfortunate that some of them contracted malaria. The mosquitoes were so thick around the pool at Colegio Ward in Ramos Mejîa in Argentina, that swimming was out of the question.

On one trip to Chanchamayo in Peru, Enrique Balloch and I found lodging in what was called a hotel. It was a red boarded-up building with cracks between the upright planks. The mosquito netting was so filthy that one could hardly breathe. Balloch decided to let the mosquitoes bite, but I suffered under the netting. There was no way to lock the door. Then about 1 or 2 a.m. someone came into our room, claiming that it was his room. He was intoxicated and it took a while for us to oust him. It was a miserable night in a primitive jungle area. There was no bath or toilet, so that made the hotel less than Class A.

Neither America is free from the insects which can become serious problems. A scientist has said long after the age of dinosaurs and of man, the next invaders to control the world would be insects. Some of you may have to keep scratching or find some other solutions. And I have just mentioned two of those "bichos" which are prevalent in all the Americas.

POSTAL IRREGULARITIES?

In recent weeks and months attention has been called to some of the irregularities and inefficiency of the postal service in the United States. That seems to be one of the problems I remember from years ago. I can recall a time in Bolivia in the 1940s when the postal service was very inefficient. In fact, it was so serious that we began to cancel the stamps with our own school seal before we deposited the mail at the local post office. It became necessary to do that because we found that the stamps were removed from the letters by the postal employees and the letters never left the post office. The stamps could then be resold and the money kept in his own pocket. If the letter did leave the post office, it did not go to the proper destination. Perhaps some other employee removed the stamps along the way. It is hard for any country to operate when there is no confidence in the postal service.

I've been hearing lately of loads of mail being discarded and never sent to its destination. I remember once in Lima in the 1950s they found a whole truckload of mail, bags and all, out on the beach and near the Pacific Ocean, which, of course, was not the original destination for which it had been designed. It took a while to get accustomed to a difficult situation which occurred down there much earlier evidently than it has come to this country.

NAME THAT TUNE

During the noon hours in Buenos Aires, one would find large crowds of men standing on the street in front of a record store which would be playing one opera or another or other classical music. Music itself was of special interest to the people and I was amazed how they could identify the different movements of the classical world, naming all the different parts of operas and symphonic music, just as their counter parts in North America would be able to tell you the batting average of baseball players or the ERA of the pitchers. Of course, this was years ago, when we still had baseball.

I thought it quite amazing that the early settlers had made a special effort to bring their music with them. They had brought their pianos and other instruments across the Andes by horse drawn carts. Some of those pianos must have been crated in Spain, shipped across the ocean, and then hauled over the mountains and had been kept in tune and in good repair for scores of years. Their descendants' appreciation of fine music must have come over in their genes. They seemed to have music in their souls. Even in the cities and towns of the interior of South America when an announcement was made that there would be a piano recital at a downtown theater, scores and even hundreds of people would attend. The performers did not have to be well known artists from another country. Local talent would also attract large audiences to hear good music even though not always elegantly or perfectly performed. The people in Bolivia seemed to have a deep appreciation of art and music.

Going to an opera or attending a concert of classical music in the great theaters, such as the Colon in Buenos Aires, was an opportunity not to be missed and envied by those who could not attend. They were very expressive in approving or disapproving the performance. If the music was very good and the singer did an exceptional job, they would applaud and even cheer as if they were at a bull fight and would shout "Olé!" On the contrary, if the singer did not put himself into the role or if there were some sour notes in the performance, they would begin to make a lot of noise, stamping their feet, which was their way of jeering the singer and expressing their disapproval of the way the music was being sung. Although at times I was not impressed as much as they were, I did admire their real appreciation for music and the artistic.

Another matter which I found very interesting, was that many of the lads in Buenos Aires who were in the YMCA for which I was supposed to be a sort of counselor, had meetings every week or two in one of the homes and would have a song fest. They would sing all kinds of favorite songs, in their own language, plus a lot of the popular songs which came from the U.S.A. They seemed to enjoy being in each others company. No women were there, just the lads from the "Y" who got together for an evening to talk as young men would, mainly about sports, or girls, but their main purpose was just to sing.

We noticed that the young people in our schools in Cochabamba were quick to learn the steps and movements of the folk games we introduced. They seemed to have a "feel" for it. In many instances it seemed they would catch on quicker than had their counterparts in the U.S.

One evening in Cochabamba we attended a concert when all of a sudden I noticed that one of the dogs, a pet of one of our resident teachers, was under my feet. The dog didn't seem to have that same appreciation for music. It became such a distraction that I felt obliged to take the pet out of the theater. I was a bit embarrassed as I had to drag Jerry down the aisle and face the others who remained to enjoy the rest of the program.

IN A MANNER OF SPEAKING (with tongue in cheek)

One usually tries to get things said in the way in which he will best be understood.

I recall a young man who came to Peru to teach and as colleagues we wondered how to pronounce his name. The Anglo spelling was easy: It was "Pate." The local people weren't sure if they should use the Anglo PATE like in "hate" or should they use the Spanish phonetic and pronounce it as in "potty", or should they give it a French version as in "Paté de foie gras" or goose liver. I think the former two were used more frequently. Well, what is in a name or in a word?

One knows that the Spanish letter "o" is always pronounced as the letter is pronounced in saying it. Yet with Anglo phonetics we think that the golfer "Chi Chi" must be called Rodriques, like the connecting rods of a car even though Spanish phonetics would demand an "o" sound as in "roe". North Americans assume the Italian singer, Pavorotti, must necessarily have "rotten" as a part of his surname.

We convince ourselves that all languages should have an English pronunciation and meaning. There are so many words which we are positive should mean the same in every language. We hear the word "constipado" in Spanish and think that the individual must be given a laxative, when actually the word only means that the person may only feel a little "under the weather." Now you must explain to another person of a different language background how to "be under the weather."

I am convinced that many gringos would prefer to have Hispanics mispronounce their native language and apply the rules of English grammar and pronunciation instead. If the North American does not understand the Spanish, he may ask for it to be repeated, and again to speak a little louder, and then he may suggest that the Hispanic should learn English. It is so much easier to understand. Even the children here in the U.S. speak it. With tongue in cheek one can say that it is easier for them to learn English than for us to learn Spanish. We are true blue monolinguals who are proud of our use of the Queen's English in the good old U.S.A, and wish that English should be spoken correctly.

Many business people think it is easier to hire English speaking help than to try to learn the language of the country where they may be working. Some also think that if they are not understood, all they need to do is to increase the volume. Some North American tourists will swear or curse someone, forgetting that foul language shouted in any language, can be understood.

It is so easy to misuse a word in another language, especially when one is so sure that one knows what it means when it is similar in spelling or pronunciation. An interim principal of a school in Bolivia in order to impress everyone at the first staff meeting, introduced members, new and old. He was doing fine until he came to one of the very senior members of the group, a dignified lady music teacher with broad credentials from studies in Europe etc. He meant to say, "Now I want to present the teacher who has been here the longest ("antigua") but he slipped by saying the most "antecuada" (antiquated) member of the staff. In that sense it was all too true, and the entire group first stifled and then broke out in a loud guffaw of laughter.

I recall how on one occasion I was trying to introduce a speaker who had a gift of real oratory who had been invited to give a talk. I wanted to say a "silvery tongued speaker," but what I ended up saying was that he was very "fácil con la palabra" which carried more the meaning "slippery tongued.

Then there is that often misused word embarrassed ("embarazado") which means "pregnant" which of course is pregnant with possibilities of error.

I recall a taxi driver in Lima one day discussing politics. He was hoping to see some political leader who would say "sí" to the right and "no" to the wrong. He then complained that in his country it was always "Sí, no", "sí, no" (yes, no, yes, no,) and never a definite "sí" to what was correct or a strong "NO" to what was wrong. He was searching for a kind of integrity which would satisfy his dreams. It is easy to insist ones ideas are the only ones to be thought correct. A small publication came across my desk in New York in the 1970s which read "Much<u>o</u> graci<u>as</u>." I called telling the writer that the gender and person should agree in Spanish and that it should correctly read, “muchas gracias.” The response was that he had called Berlitz and they had assured him that he was right. I knew that it was wrong, but who could argue with him if he had assumed wrongly that he had heard correctly from Berlitz. My friend was happy with his own mistaken arrogance. What's in a word? It all depends.

I once took part in a Guaraní Bible translation conference in Paraguay. A local university professor posed as the authority, but rather than include an occasional Spanish word like "mesa" (table) in his work, he would manufacture a word which he thought ought to be a part of the Guaraní language. We called several Paraguayan teachers to read his translation, but they could not since the supposed authority, a native of the country, had made up so many words that they could not understand what had been written, although it was supposedly in their native tongue. It is the people who determine the flow of a language.

Many "modismos" or idiomatic expressions seem better in other languages than in English. We like to kid or tease someone, and say that they are pulling one's leg. In Spanish, however, the oft used expression "tomando el pelo" (pulling one's hair), is more realistic than "pulling one's leg" (except for a bald person.)

These illustrations reinforce the value of knowledge of a word and how it can change one's meaning or purpose. In a manner of speaking it can make all the difference in the world. So what's in a word? We all play the word game to a degree. It can be an educational or a very sobering experience.

LANGUAGES

Portuguese is the language of Brazil and Spanish is the official language of the rest of the countries of South America except for Paraguay which uses both Spanish and Guarani. There are many Indian languages spoken and one heard a lot of Italian and German in Argentina. Word differences between countries are greater than language differences. Pronunciation also differed but it was more like the variations found in the different sections of the United States.

In northern Uruguay one finds a small city known as "Chuy." The main street of the town runs along the border with Brazil. The business signs on one side of the street are in Spanish and on the other side they are in Portuguese. They seem to have no problem with bilingualism. Passersby spend more time comparing prices and rates of exchange than in language differences.

Each country has its own vocabulary. There are different words for fruits and vegetables. Pineapple is "piña" in most countries, but in some it is "anana." In some of the countries "vainitas" are green beans but in others they are known as "chauchas". Beets are either "beterragas" or "remolachas." The verb "coger" means to "catch" or "to pick up" in most countries but in others it means to rape and one must use "agarrar" instead.

In some countries auto tires are called "llantas." In Brazil they were called "pneumaticos" or "pneus." In some countries they are called "Gomas" (rubbers). A contraceptive is known as a "preservativo."

Similar languages can cause some interesting variations. In Peru, for example a "pavo" is a turkey, whereas in Brazil a turkey is known as a "peru." In North America some humans are known as turkeys, but that is a different kind of fowl.

THIS AND THAT

Telling Time

That other America seems to prefer the military system of telling the hours of the day or night. A meeting will begin at "veinte horas," or at 20 hours which means 8 p.m. That avoided any concern as to whether it meant a.m. or p.m.

Metric System

The metric system was also more commonly used than in North America. One measured distances by centimeters, meters, kilometers etc. One of the lads in the school was quite short and he carried the nickname of "Metro", even though he was a bit taller than that.

One advantage in travel was that one could drive along at 100 kilometers per hour and still be within our speed limit, knowing that 100 kms. was approximately 60 miles per hour. The metric system seems far superior or at least simpler, and someday it may become common place in North America.

Occasionally one did hear references to that wonderful English system. For example, an inch width was called a "pulgada", based on the word "pulgar" which is the thumb in Spanish. Historically the thumb was thought to be an inch wide ("mas o menos") (more or less).

Your Name

In South America a male has not only a given name and the father's surname, but also the mother's maiden name. For example, Juan

Morales Olivas. His father's name is Morales but his mother's maiden name was Olivas.

A woman bears her father's name and her mother's name until she is married and then adds "de " her husband's name. The "de," meaning "of" or that she belongs to her husband, although the bonds may not necessarily mean that much. For example, Mary Smith Makay de Frankfort (if her husband's name is Frankfort). If he predeceases her she will be known as Mary Smith Makay, "viuda" (widow) de Frankfort.

Hot Water

Some one told me that she had almost scalded herself in the shower when she turned the faucet to "C" for cold only to remember painfully that that letter meant "caliente"

Hot or Cold

Few homes had central heating. The usual source of heating in Argentina was called "quebracho", a wood which was too heavy to float and burned like anthracite coal. One could stoke a fire in a fire place, and it would still be burning the following morning. Our heating system in Buenos Aires (Acassuso) was ineffective. There was a nice fireplace in the living-dining room area which had a radiator inside at the back of it. The radiator was supposed to get hot enough from the fire in the fireplace and was then to transfer the heat to the radiators in the other parts of the house. The system did not work. There never was enough heat in the other rooms to make any noticeable difference. We would buy the "quebracho" by truck loads, never sure if the scale being used was weighing in pounds or kilos. We were not comfortably warm until natural gas was supplied to our suburb and we purchased a gas heater. South of the Equator July and August were the coldest months. In Buenos Aires, we would have a frost two or three times during the winter. An occasional front, however, made it seem quite cold and damp, and we were always convinced that the whole question of temperature was relative. Temperature was measured in centigrade. A reading of 20 degrees Centigrade seemed colder than 68 degrees Fahrenheit.

How High is Up, When is One Down?

One of the first times coming down on an elevator in South America, I punched "1" and got off to leave the building, only to discover that I was still up a floor. I didn't see a "G" but someone said to punch P.B. which I was told meant "planta baja", or low floor. It is a good thing they didn't have any sub-basement stops or I might still be underground in that other America.

High, of course, could refer to the mountains of the Andes for that other America does have the higher ones. Aconcagua is the highest and Illimani in Bolivia is like a sentinel looking over La Paz. I was told that the highest ski resort in the world was on the slopes of Illimani. The air is thin up there but at ski speed one would feel that there was more air from the rushing speed of the wind, although there would be no more oxygen.

Street Children

Another common sight was the number of beggars on the streets, often children who were taught to add to the family income by begging or selling lottery tickets. One trick was to drop a "huachito" or lottery ticket at ones feet while walking by and then claiming that destiny or fate had caused him to drop that lucky ticket at our feet to prove that it must be a winning number.

Service People

Just as was also the case in the U.S. many years ago, in Buenos Aires in the 1960s, a meat man would come by the house in the afternoon to take orders for the meat we would need for the next day. He would then return the following day and deliver the order. The baker or "panadero" would come around and ring his bell, like a Good Humor man, so people could come out and buy the hard crusted unwrapped bread he had to offer. He did not carry pastries on the wagon. Many of these service people used the horse and buggy and horses were required by law to be provided with "hats" to protect them from the heat in the summer timc.

WHERE TO?

Transportation to other cities in Peru in the 1940s was available by train, plane, or bus. While we were in Peru some enterprising people had initiated a station wagon or limousine service which would take one from one's home to one's destination in a major city and that was a great improvement. The last was more expensive, but this taxi service was quite good. If the condition of the roads had been better, one might say that the service was excellent. Busses were the worst, since they were crowded with people, chickens, ducks, small children and tons of luggage. It is no wonder that they were always breaking down. Many of the Indians with their families and their belongings would be crowded or jammed into the back of a truck, as they travelled from one place to another. It was rather common to read of a bus that had toppled off a mountain road with few if any survivors. Small crosses were used along the side of the road instead of guard rails. They were good reminders to drive slowly, but not always effective.

Getting a driver's license in itself was something of a problem. The eye test was rather difficult. One had to allign two objects at a distance by pulling some wires through a small orifice. As someone said, it was almost like getting a brevet for flying a plane. Some of our friends had quite a bit of difficulty in getting their license. The real advantage was that once one had the license one could drive "as he pleased", almost like "Jehu." It was also good to have a working claxon or horn.

Many thought it was more important than the brakes. It didn't seem to me that they enforced the traffic laws as much as they do in this country, but usually people managed to get to their destination without too much difficulty.

At the time gasoline ("nafta") was only about 10 cents for a U.S. gallon. Once one could afford a car, the operation was quite cheap. I even saw a small VW bug chauffered, with the owner sitting in a crowded back seat. The salary of the chauffeur was very reasonable compared to the price of the car.

Transportation in thc city of Lima was also aided by the use of old touring cars which travelled the streets of Lima on designated routes. They were known as "colectivos". There seemed to be no limit to the number of passengers these old cars could carry. They charged little and were always filled to capacity and beyond. Of course, a taxi could take one in solitary company to one's destination.

Another way to get there was to climb atop or hang on to the sides of the "tranvía" (street car) especially on the nine kilometer ride to Callao. Surely this is no longer done. I admit that I never tried the "hang" method.

Driving across the Andes was always an experience. One had to be sure to have the carburator adjusted just right in order to get enough gas to adapt to the altitude

We were to have a meeting in Huancayo.

The road was under repair from recent mud slides and traffic was closed during the day. John Shappel called suggesting that we leave Lima and drive at night. We were on the high point of the pass at Ticlio, and were trailing a truck. After signaling that we wanted to pass, we saw the driver of the truck put his head out of the window, motioning that we could pass. However, just about the time we were parallel with the truck, the driver gently sideswiped our car, nudging us to the edge of that mountain road. Two wheels of our car were off the road. The road was gravel, and there was no way to get back on the road without help. At that altitude, it was cold standing there waiting for another car to come. After a few calls for help were ignored, one truck was kind enough to stop. He had a rope and a chain and after a few attempts he was able to jerk us back onto the road. We had lost the door handles on the side of the car. We were thankful to be once again on our way and not at the bottom of the mountain side.

A trip by car or station wagon or bus down into the valley of Chanchamayo was always an adventure. The road was one lane wide, and little crosses planted along the way indicated where others had not made it and had toppled down the mountain side into oblivion. The road had no guard rails. The rule was that traffic was supposed to go down one day and up the next. The problem was that people would forget and try the wrong way on wrong days. Occasionally there was a space wide enough to allow cars to pass, but those were few and far between. I noticed that the passengers on a bus were friendly and talkative as the trip began. Then there would be a long period of silence when we passed through the most dangerous, steepest and curviest part of the trip. As we approached either the top or the bottom, all seemed to breathe a sign of relief and again became quite jovial and noisy. On one trip I asked how far it was to the bottom of the gorge. Someone answered that it was 200 feet, which was quite a drop. We weren't sure, but someone said that "a couple hundred of feet wouldn't make much difference!" Perhaps the periods of silence were spent in prayer. I can still see those little crosses along the side of the road and am thankful to be alive.

When some visitors to the United States returned they said they were impressed by the order of things in the U.S. Drivers usually drove in lanes, and they even had signs along the highways indicating where deer could cross the road!

Travel in Bolivia was quite similar to that in Peru, but always complicated. At that time in 1945 there was no road between the major cities of Cochabamba and La Paz, Bolivia.

ALL ABOARD!

In most of South America the train service was built by the British. There was a clamor for nationalization since many were convinced the British were making too much money from the railroads. Even later, with local ownership, the on time performance was questioned. "On time" was translated "hora Inglesa" (English time) and that began to happen with less regularity. The trip from Cochabamba to La Paz was originally 12 to 14 hours but when we were there in 1945 it had increased to about 20 hours. In the section between Cochabamba and La Paz there are many switch backs, (or as they say, zig-zags) to gain altitude. For some unknown reason the train would approach a station and then charge on through for a couple of kilometers, stop suddenly and then back up and return to the station. We would back up until we hit the barriers at faster than expected speeds and receive a bouncy jolt. Fortunately, the barriers held. As passengers we wondered what was going on, since it was not a one time occurrence but continued all day. The next day the newspapers gave us an explanation. The engineer and crew had been inebriated. We were glad when we reached La Paz and then took the "Internacional" to head south. We had a very interesting trip on the way to Argentina. Long stops were made at each station. Someone suggested that the crew was possibly greeting some women friends. In fact, during the interval, I had time to take a taxi ride to see the "town" on more than one occasion.

The train from Lima to Huancayo, Peru, one of the highest standard gauge railroads, crosses the Andes at a pass at the town of Ticlio, which is at an altitude of about 15,800 feet. Mountain sickness called "soroche" in some places and "puma" in others, can make one so sick, nauseous and weak that one thinks the end has come. At other times it isn't so bad. Once when we came back from Argentina, Lorla felt so weak that she could not raise her arms up to fix her hair. I had to help hold them up enough so she could manage to get the job done and look fairly presentable. A little trainman with a goatskin bag of oxygen and bellows would walk down the aisles of the train, and upon seeing someone about to pass out from oxygen deficiency, would start pumping the bellows. That was sometimes described as the "lifeline" of the Andes. I occasionally needed a breath of oxygen to revive me and I was not alone. "Soroche" is very unpleasant and can be fatal at times, although only once per person.

One of the most unpleasant trips over the Andes by train included a "trasbordo." Our friends, the Lewellens, from St. Louis were with us to enjoy the experience. The Lewellens were probably in their mid or late sixties at the time, but we were never quite certain of their age. I decided to take Sally, our daughter, (who was then about four or five) with us on the trip. The train left Lima about 7 a.m.

We had been warned about the "aluvión" (mud slide)) but were informed that the delay would not be serious. We made it to the pass at Ticlio, more or less on schedule. Sally had become very ill with "soroche". The attendant with a goat skin bag of oxygen came around to pump a few breaths of oxygen into her face, but Sally was so ill that there was little or no noticeable benefit. She was so ill from "vómitos" and loss of blood that we were concerned for her safety but there was nothing we could do at that point. Shortly afterwards the train stopped and the trainmen shouted "Trasbordo". Everyone was ordered off the train to start walking to reach another train which had come from Huancayo to meet us and was waiting to take us to our destination. It was quite an ordeal to walk through that mud carrying our luggage. Sally was too sick to walk, so Cecil volunteered to carry her on his shoulders as we trudged through that mud—which was about six inches deep in the shallowest part. We were informed that the walk would be about two kilometers, but it seemed like miles. It was an unusual sight to see that mass of humanity slipping and sliding and struggling through all that distance with their luggage, children and other belongings, but we finally did see the other train on the other side of the mud slide. We arrived in Huancayo after dark, several hours late.

I told our friends that they couldn't take a trip like that in the U.S. at any price. "No," Cecil said, "nor would I want to". We had mud on our shoes and clothes. I was just thankful that the mudslide did not occur while we were trudging to the other train or even while we were on the train, since trains can be carried down a mountain side with more serious consequences to the passengers. The Lewellens stayed at a hotel in Huancayo but Sally and I stayed with friends at the mission residence. We made it through the night. The next day the adults toured the city and surrounding area before heading back to Lima the following day. Sally was still sick, but once we got down to 10,000 feet elevation she began to feel better. By the time we reached Lima that evening she was jumping around but feeling weak from the loss of blood and nourishment. I did not plan to take a trip again if I knew in advance there was to be a "trasbordo."

I made the trip from Lima to Huancayo over the Andes many times. The train passes through 65 tunnels between Chosica and Huancayo. Some of these great train rides have been shown on public television, but one has to take the trip to appreciate the adventure and to get the effect of the smoke filled tunnels, and the fresh air and bright sunlight when one emerges from them.

In 1946 we were required to get out of the altitude in Bolivia and to spend some time at sea level. We went to Antofagasta, Chile. From La Paz the train headed South to Uyuni. It was very dusty because one crosses the Atacama desert (said to be the driest in the world). In the diner the table cloth was so covered with sand that when one picked up a spoon, the mark of the spoon was very visible. There are also volcanoes in the area. The abundance of oxygen at sea level was wonderful.

Overnight travel meant that you got off the train and spent a night in a hotel, and then reboarded in the morning, or on the "internacional one either had a "compartment" or traveled second or third class and rode all night on wooden benches.

I found it difficult to travel by train in Argentina when there was a "huelga" (strike). I had a speaking engagement, and I was warned that the train would be late, since a slow down said they would travel two hours, and rest or be idle for one. That went on all day. The last stoppage left me still an hour from my destination. While they stopped, I made a call to let my hosts know where I was. They drove out to get me and take me to the meeting.

It was strange to find a large railway station in the shape of a locomotive just east of Cochabamba, especially since there were no tracks. Plans had been made to connect with the main railroad going to Santa Cruz and on to Corumbá to Brazil. It was a grandiose idea, the magnificent station was built, and a few kilometers of track were laid before the project was abandoned for lack of funds. It reminded me of some people who seem to be all station and no tracks, getting and going nowhere.

In spite of all the inconveniences, the railroads have been a great boost for South America as well as for North America.

COME FLY WITH ME

It is probably the airplane that has brought the different areas of South America into closer proximity. In fact, the air lines have helped the countries become viable as functioning units. In Bolivia, Lloyd Aereo Boliviano rendered a great service to the country, especially for domestic travel, and Panagra or Pan American Grace served the international area. In Peru, a real pioneer was Elmer "Slim" Fawcett. After military service, Fawcett started his airline in Peru. At first he was ridiculed since there were crashes until some wondered if he would have enough planes left for service. I visited with Elmer Fawcett when he had his office in the Hotel Bolívar in Lima. He was a Kentuckian and was pleased to tell one how proud he was. The little oxygen tubes used in planes were more sophisticated than the goatskin bags used on the trains.

Our first trip down to Cochabamba in 1945 took us 23 days by plane. We flew in a cargo plane from New Orleans to Mérida in the Yucatan peninsula. After being rudely awakened by a cup of super black coffee ("espreso"), we were transferred to a DC 3, stopping at each of the Central American capitals before being off loaded in Panama. It was war time and not having reservations until days later, we had to return each day while impatiently waiting for a vacancy. The next leg of the journey took us to Cali, Colombia. Then a flight to Lima, Peru left us stranded again. At last, a flight took us to Arequipa, Peru, and then on to La Paz and Cochabamba, Bolivia.

I recall one flight on which we had boarded the plane, finding it crowded with people. It must have had 60-80 people on that DC3, over twice the normal capacity. I was sure that the plane would never get off the ground with that much of an overload. I was pleased when one of the stewards announced, “Everyone off the plane who doesn't have a ticket.” There was quite an exodus, and I breathed a sigh of relief, as half the crowd departed. We still had the normal number of passengers. The rules were different. One had to say farewell or good bye to one's friends. I am sure that many of those people had never flown on a plane, but they had certainly been on planes many times.

CITIES

A year ago a friend of ours was going to make a trip to Buenos Aires and wanted some ideas as to what he might do when he was there. We prepared a three page list of things to do and see in Argentina. We suggested the famous Colón Opera house in Buenos Aires. It is quite an institution with its scores of full time employees who are there to make the scenery, tailors and seamstresses to make the costumes, and the musicians and all those who participate in the production of an opera. The famous stars that perform in La Scala in Milan and other great opera houses in the world, also perform in the Teatro Colón in Buenos Aires. I suggested he might take a short trip out to the countryside to see an "hacienda" or a ranch because Argentina is famous for its cattle or beef. Then I mentioned other places he might want to visit. Upon his return I asked him how much of the list he had seen. It was almost nothing. He had only been there for two or three days and Buenos Aires is now a city of approximately eleven million inhabitants, and one cannot really appreciate the extent of that metropolis in such a short time.

Buenos Aires, referred to as B.A., is sometimes called the Paris of South America. It is a beautiful cosmopolitan city, with wide avenues, fountains at many intersections, many parks, like Palermo, and many statues and monuments to commemorate historical events such as "El Cabildo," the "Casa Rosada," “El Congreso," and the " Palacio de Justicia." There are many modern buildings as well as museums and art galleries—a city which is expressive of its varied cultures.

At an international meeting in Rio de Janeiro, Brazil, in the 1960s, many of the delegates were from the United States. One man was impressed by the extent and the beauty of the city. He asked me from where I had come, and when I replied, Buenos Aires, Argentina, he said, "You mean there is another town south of here?" He thought Rio was as far south as one could go. He thought the rest of South America was mostly jungle. Geography certainly is not one of the strong points of some North Americans. As far as they are concerned there is no place like the U.S.A. and its superior qualities.

Then, of course, there are cities like Sao Paulo, Brazil, which is famous for its architecture. It was designed by a German architect. I think his name was Niemeyer. Most visitors are surprised by its skyscrapers and modernity.

Bahía on the coast of Brazil has an excellent view of the ocean and is also another large city. Although one of the general problems in South America is that it is under populated, you will discover that the cities are very crowded. That alone causes many problems as it does in cities everywhere.

Brazilia, the new capital of Brazil, is a modern city planned and designed in advance and still one gets the impression that it was built in too much of a hurry. It still has a lot to do to become the city it was intended to be.

Lima, Peru is known as the "City of Kings". It was founded on January 6th, the day of the Kings or magi. Montevideo, Uruguay, Santiago in Chile, Carracas, Venezuela, and Bogotá, Colombia, are other cities typical of those to be found in that other America, and many more have historical relevance.

For anyone, who has the time, the wherewithal and the energy to travel, I would recommend that he visit the cities to the south and discover that the continent is not all jungle. There are many beautiful areas and very modern cities. I think you will probably find more bidets in South American bathrooms than you will find in North American cities. That doesn't make them any more superior but it does suggest that they do have some areas of progress or development.

If you do have a chance to go to South America, spend more than a weekend there. It just can't be covered in a few days. Brazil alone is an area larger than the U.S. and Argentina is as large as that part of the U.S. east of the Mississippi. My concern is that many times North Americans who spend only a few days there come back to the U.S. and pose as authorities, speaking of the people and of under development and miss the significant historical heritage as well as the dreams for the future which are present in that other America.

CHUBUT VALLEY

The Welsh settled quite a large area of Middle Argentina extending from Puerto Madryn on or near the East coast all the way across to the Andes. Richard Llewellyn (of "How Green Was My Valley" fame) spent a year or two in the Chubut valley. He wrote about his experience in a book called "Up into the Singing Mountain."

Llewellyn claimed that the purest Welsh in the world was still spoken by the Welsh settlers in the Chubut valley. Since much of the area was semi-arid, those Welsh pioneers, who had been miners, brought their picks and shovels along with them. They dug irrigation ditches across the country in order to make the desert blossom like a rose. They were very hard working, independent pioneers. They carried on their Welsh tradition of hymn singing and music competitions just as they had back in Wales.

The governor of the province was a friend who sent out someone to meet me at the airport, and made me feel like a guest of honor. It was interesting to meet all the Morgans, Roberts, Williams, Jones and Davis and other familiar Welsh names.

I always enjoyed visiting the Chubut valley and the state or province bearing the same name. I can't vouch for the purity of the Welsh language spoken in Argentina, but I can confirm that they have kept their traditional values, and are an industrious people who have made an excellent contribution to their new home in Argentina. They have been there for over 150 years.

BARILOCHE

There are places of exquisite beauty in both Americas. One could mention the canyons, the geysers and parks of North as well as South America. One of real beauty in that other America is the lake region of Argentina and Chile, the area around San Carlos de Bariloche. Those lakes and mountains are as beautiful as any to be found anywhere in the world. They said that Lake Nahuel Huapi is 800 meters deep. The water is too cold for swimming but is so pure and clean that it is used directly in the potable water system of the town of San Carlos. I didn't even question it. The reflection of the shoreline on the water is mirrored clearly.

Hotel Llao Llao was a beautiful hotel in the 1960s. The golf courses were excellent. President Ike Eisenhower used to go down to that lake region for golf and fishing. On one occasion we rented a boat which was piloted by a Captain Beckman. It was a new experience to troll with 200-300 yards of line behind the boat. Our youngest daughter caught the only fish we caught that day. It was a very good lake trout. I don't know how much it weighed, but Gerda prepared it on the top of the sizzling red hot cook stove. It was delicious and eight of us enjoyed an excellent meal.

The other aspects of vacation life are wonderful. One can enjoy winter sports such as skiing during the months of June- August as the seasons are reversed south of the equator.

This area is sometimes called the Switzerland of South America. Many settlers have come there from Switzerland and Germany and have brought their own type of architecture with them.

FISH STORIES

Two maids from the secondary school in Cochabamba stood at my door. They said that some North American men had been fishing in the streams up the mountain and had caught some nice trout. The Dicksons were offering to share some of the catch with us. It sounded so wonderful. Then the girls said that their cook at the secondary school could fix them "muy rico" and would we like her to prepare them for us. Since our cooking facilities at the primary school where we lived were very limited, we agreed. We waited and waited, our taste buds salivating in anticipation. Hours later they were back. The fish had been boiled and we were greeted with fish "mush". Lorla said she never dreamed that anyone would think of preparing those trout in such a manner. What a disappointment, we felt like crying.

I had a speaking engagement in Rio Gallegos, in the southern part of Argentina in the 1960s. A banker in the town asked me to go fishing with him. He had all the equipment and I had the desire to catch a fish. The fishing was great. The banks were not too high, the ground level, so one could simply cast out into the river and catch a fish. We caught several nice fish. I had never fished before with such success. It seemed that this was virgin territory, at least as far as the fish were concerned. One barely threw a line in the water when one had a fish. It was so much fun we kept thinking we would just get one more. They weighed four to five pounds each. It was so enjoyable that we didn't realize how much time had past. In fact, when we finally got to the meeting we learned that we were late, the dinner was over and red-faced I tried to apologize

Yet, I had all those fish (a half dozen or more) and made a major mistake of trying to salt them in order to preserve them for the trip back to Buenos Aires. The problem was that we overdid it. By the time we reached home, the fish were too salty to use at all! That was a bitter disappointment, but I still remember that afternoon in the southern Argentine countryside.

AMAZON

Having lived along the Mississippi for years I always had a desire to see the Amazon. That opportunity came when a friend working at the U.S Embassy invited me to go with him to visit that area. Dusty was a specialist in insecticides who was going to Iquitos, Peru, to give some advice to managers and workers on a farm project sponsored by the Peruvian government.

To begin farming the local people would just cut down the trees and let them rot where they fell. In that way something was added to the thin top soil, since the abundance of rain bleached the soil and washed much of it into and down the river. This was about forty years ago. The local farm workers were trying to develop a good forage crop to feed the beginning of a dairy herd. They had grown a field of alfalfa and kudzu, but the cows weren't producing enough milk to make the project feasible. In fact, having lived in Southern Minnesota before going to South America, I was surprised to find some cans of evaporated milk from the Rochester, Minnesota Dairy Co-op there in Iquitos. Army ants were very destructive. This was one of Leonard's opportunities to help. We asked what the local people had done. We were told that they would fill the holes and tunnels of the ants with crude oil and gasoline and ignite it. "Did it help eliminate the problem?" The reply was, "It didn't get rid of the ants, but it did slow them down."

We stayed with a friend named Phil and we spent a wonderful and informative week during the "Carnaval" period. I even met a man from St. Louis, Missouri who lived in a house built on stilts to avoid flooding and provided an excellent place for diving into their front yard pool of water in at least part of the year if they were not concerned about the "piranhas", the flesh eating fish. Because of the water level, even the cemeteries had to be above ground.

We were most impressed by the people, learning that they were quite a mixture, having their origins from many parts of the world. Some came from German and French backgrounds and many other nations were represented. Some of their ancestors had been attracted by the search for rubber. "Fordlandia" had been one of those projects. Then during the war period, some had been employed by the Rubber Development Corp. (RDC) which was in the area to develop another source for rubber, since the Pacific areas were closed, and there was a shortage. The miscegenation process had produced some very handsome people. Many of the women walked so beautifully and had excellent carriage. They carried things on their head which developed excellent posture. They seemed to glide along as they walked. We were especially impressed by the two young maids in Phil's house, since they were topless. Any mistaken ideas were soon obliterated when we saw them skillfully prepare the meat and vegetables for the meals as they wielded their machetes.

The Amazon climate is warm, and we noticed that quite a few of the women were scantily clad as they did their laundry seated beside a stream. The abundance of water and the tropical climate seemed to encourage frequent bathing and a fair degree of cleanliness.

One day we took a hike into the jungle area, carrying machetes. We walked on our way for a few minutes, sometimes we walked on cut logs which formed the path, until we came to a small river which flowed into the Amazon. As these streams were infested with the "Piranha" fish, our expedition ended rather quickly. We felt ill equipped for a jungle safari.

On another day we were taken to a shed or barnlike building to witness a human auction. About eight or ten Indians were seated on the ground awaiting their fate. Their hair had been cut, possibly guided by a bowl. I pointed to one of the Indians, and he pointed back at me smiling. For him I was the odd one. My friend and I neither bid nor bought. I later read that a commission of the United Nations had passed a resolution that all people were to refrain from and desist from engaging in this practice. I can still see those lads who had been captured and were being sold, especially the one who looked and pointed at me knowing that for him I was the odd looking character. And I admit that he looked more related to the environment than I did.

One day during "carnaval" (the period just prior to Lent) we saw a group of very spirited Indians, augmented by additional spirits consumed, dancing around a "piñata." The goodies were placed higher and almost out of reach. Only by using a machete could it be brought down. Bottles of beer and other prizes kept them clamoring and dancing around the post in the mud. When at last the prizes came down, there was a mad scramble to retrieve them. Then we were guided down into the port area known as "Belem" (Bethlehem). I was aware of the custom during carnaval of throwing bags or balloons of water or whatever (including urine). At one corner they were singing and dancing and a high time seemingly being enjoyed. Phil encouraged us to go into the hall but I thought it unwise. He said, "They won't bother us since we are gringos. These were famous last words. They were really inventing their own approach to what today might be called "dirty dancing." Some were obviously copulating as a part of the dance. I was suddenly struck by an improvised bag made from an intestine and I was splattered with some foul smelling and colorful liquid, the stains of which it took several weeks of washing to remove. We thought it prudent to run out of Belem as quickly as possible.

On another day we rented a boat, a side-wheeler with the pilot captain and a crew of one to explore the river. We went down the Itaya, a tributary, and then out on the big river, the Amazon. We felt like kings as we gave orders as to where we wanted to go and what to see. There were occasional villages along the way. We didn't quite dare to go ashore. I had never seen such a vast forest or jungle area. No wonder it is known as the "green hell" and I was sure that once stranded there I would never be able to hack my way out through such dense vegetation. The Amazon seemed like more than a river. I was far inland. The river drains over two million square miles of land. I felt very small out there. I remembered having read about Tom Harmon, a one time Michigan football great, getting lost and fighting his way out of the jungle, but I knew that I was in no condition to do such battle even if necessary. I had read about the great impact this area had on the climate of millions of square kilometers, but I was more interested in the people and the culture of those who were making their own life style. I felt so helpless on that two-decker side-wheeler.

I wanted to fish for one of those big "dorado" game fish for which the river was famous, but I didn't have any adequate equipment. Even if I caught one, I knew the line would never hold. After all, I wanted to catch one of those "big ones". We just felt fortunate that the exchange rate was as favorable as it was to afford us such an excellent opportunity to visit the area.

My friend, the specialist in insecticides, did not see a great future in agriculture or in dairy development without destroying the natural evolution of the area. The battle still rages over the use of that great basin. Should it have its natural role in affecting the weather, or should exploitation for financial gain eventually destroy the potential? That was in 1948. The battle continues, even producing martyrs for a cause.

Undoubtedly Iquitos is quite a large and modern city by now. Perhaps they have destroyed those "army ants" but I doubt if all the pesky mosquitoes along the Amazon have disappeared. Even sleeping under a "mosquitero" (mosquito netting) I discovered that they could still launch an attack on me. The air was cooler and fresher without the netting, and luckily I was not infected with malaria.

I had the privilege of being a short time observer of a process which will go on indeterminately without my intervention or assistance. I was surprised to see how the people lived along the Big River and to learn of their customs during "Carnaval". Of course, for me I can still see those thinly clad women carrying produce on their heads and gliding along with such graceful carriage. This was an experience never to be forgotten.

I read recently of the arrival of some Avon ladies who were trying to sell cosmetics to those native women. Maybe that is what they need to fit into the scheme of things in our modern world. If they have no money to pay, they take vegetables or any kind of produce as barter so they can close the deal.

FENCE POSTS

Archibald MacLeish, one time librarian of congress, used to say that fence rows in Argentina were like the lines of the meridian, they were so far apart. In the 1960s one could drive along the country side and first discover that these were not modern interstate highways and be further impressed by the vast expanse of land, the cattle grazing on hundreds or thousands of acres. Startled rheas (ostriches) and jack rabbits would leap out of the pampas, and bound off towards the horizon. The rustic dwellings of the gauchos were hectares apart. Should one have the good fortune to pass near one of them one might find the hides of animals hung on lines for drying. At the right time of day one might have been invited to share in the "asado" (barbecue).

It was interesting to note that the road signs did not indicate how far it was to the next city, but each road sign noted how far one had come. On one trip with the family we headed south to go to a "Y" camp near Bahía Blanca. We followed the known highway as far as we could. We knew we needed to turn off the highway in order to go to Sierra de la Ventana but there was no indication of any road. Finally, we decided to turn anyway and followed a fence through the fields. Fortunately it was a bright sunny day but it was very dusty. We drove for miles and after a few hours came to a dirt road heading in what we hoped was the right direction and eventually, actually arrived at our destination.

We enjoyed our stay at the camp at Sierra de la Ventana. We learned to play Cropogo. This was a combination of croquet, polo and golf. The course was laid out in the hills and presented some real challenges. We prayed that it would not rain before our departure. Unfortunately, it did rain for a day or two and the stream by the camp was swollen. The fields were muddy and we had no idea how to get to a main highway. Thinking to have safety in numbers, we decided to go with another group which was leaving camp. They were going to go east until they found the main road to Mar del Plata. It was a real challenge to drive across farm land where the grain was being harvested. There was no indication of a road at all. We felt like real pioneers, although we had the advantage of a jeep station wagon rather than having to go on horseback. One of the cars had some difficulty. We waited a while as repairs were being made, but anxious to reach "civilization" we ventured on alone and we considered it good fortune to find a road which did lead to our desired destination.

Another interesting route of travel was to go from western Argentina from the town of Esquel south through the foothills of the Andes. That area was very rocky. In fact, it was so rough that a friend of ours with whom I was traveling had made arrangements with Goodyear® tire company to test some of their tires on those rough roads. They would supply the tires and he would report on the condition of the tires after so many kilometers. I could see that this road would provide an excellent test. Somehow we managed to get there and back on that rather rugged and isolated terrain.

With care, one could possibly have driven across most of the pampas and on down to Patagonia. One would have had to carry extra tires and automotive supplies to meet any kind of emergency. The towns were few and far between and one would not have found a petrol station, mechanic or even any kind of auto repair just down the road. Nor would one have found the big semis or much traffic at all. One probably could have managed to drive as far south as Rio Gallegos.

HISTORICAL LORE

Of course, everyone has heard of the Incas and their civilization. I had a wonderful time visiting the Cuzco and Machu Picchu areas. Cuzco, meaning "navel", was the life line of the Inca empire. We flew by plane to Cuzco and then took a train car down the trail to the famous Indian ruins, first uncovered by Dr. Hiram Bingham, a North American. We were surprised to learn that the Incas had performed difficult brain operations. They had developed a system of running water in their homes. They had a complicated bookkeeping system which was ably handled by the "quipus," a system of knots tied on a string. They knew how to use the plants to make dyes which even centuries later, remained still bright in color. Their communication system developed roads on which the runners sped. One wonders how they managed to get those huge bolders to fit so perfectly one on top of the others. They were accomplished in many ways. Numerous books written on the Incas would be worth the reading.

While I was in the Trujillo area of Peru, I visited the Chan Chan ruins—a pre-Incan city which has been preserved because of the arid climate. To trod down those ancient streets, just as the pre-Incans had done many centuries before, was exciting.

I also visited the private museum of the Larco Herrera family which equals the national archeological museum in Magdalena in quality and excellence.

The Nazca "flight" plans in Peru and their significance are still a mystery today.

"UNIVERSITARIOS"

It seemed to me that University students in the 1950s in Peru were a much more important factor in local politics in South America than in the U.S. Many times the "Universitarios" were the leaders in fomenting and then leading the promotion for government change. Then some political party or labor movement would support them. They were really an important factor in the political situation in South America.

Student unrest began in the secondary (high schools). The girls in their separate schools were just as adamant as were the boys. At times the students would go on strike and barricade themselves inside the building until some of their demands would be met. They would also congregate in the streets and mounted police would advance upon them until they would disperse, but not until they had expressed their defiance.

It was said that the University of Cordoba was the first autonomous university in the hemisphere. The students as well as professors approved of staff .

Although there is a bit of difference and rivalry over which is the oldest university in the Americas, we know that the University of Mexico and San Marcos in Lima, Peru are the two oldest. In fact, these two universities were making preparations to celebrate their centenaries when Harvard was just beginning its educational service (founded 1636). One should at least recognize that the other America had quite a head start.

There is no question that Harvard has the largest financial endowment but the buildings and physical equipment in those universities in that other America, have rendered a great contribution to education. Although Harvard students haven't been known as leaders in political revolutions as have their South American counterparts, one cannot deny the fact that Harvard graduates have taken a leading role in providing political and governmental leadership in the development of the United States.

THE RELIGIOUS TRADITION

The influence of Roman Catholicism is very strong in that other America. In spite of occasional complaints of shortages of priests and women religious, the influence of the Church is very apparent. One can talk to almost anyone on the street about his religion and he will say that he is "Catolico, Romano y Apostolico". Possibly he has not been to mass for years, but it is still very much a part of his tradition. He has been baptized and taken part in first communion and is usually married in the church. He is there to attend the last rites for members of his family. He may admit or say he has little to do with the church. I asked some taxi drivers about their interest in the church. One said he hadn't gone to confession since high school when he sought the priest's blessing when taking a difficult exam. Another told me that he hadn't been to a mass since the funeral of his Aunt Sofia. In general the women seem to be more devout. The "Beatas" or very religious women go to mass with a higher degree of regularity.

The externals of religion were everywhere in evidence. Public vehicles such as buses usually had a small light and a picture of a Saint by the rear view mirror as a kind of religious protection from danger. Taxi drivers also had a light bulb illuminating a Saint as a sign of religious faith. Yet when one asked if he attended mass he would say mass was for the women and children. He was too "macho" to go to church. That was a frequent response. I remember a trucker in Peru who gave a name to each of his trucks. Invoking the aid of the Omnipotent, one truck was called "Dios Poderoso Número Uno" (Almighty God Number One). Another was called "Dios Poderoso Número Dos" etc. Some of the names seemed more sacrilegious than religious. “La carnicería de la Santa Trinidad” (The butchershop of the Holy Trinity) was one. A bus line was “Jesús María" and referred to an area of the city.

Religious holidays were observed by the schools but for the most part, it was business as usual. Most enjoyed the additional holidays more as relaxation than as holy days. An exception was Good Friday. After the period of “carnavales” Holy Week was usually observed with greater dedication. Each church would take the "saints" out for an airing and viewing and to lead the procession. What struck me most at first was the use of a loud military band to keep the people moving and the use of fireworks. I recall one day trying to cross a main avenue in Lima, Peru when the Good Friday procession was in progress. I got about half way across the street when I discovered that I was moving along with the procession, unable to get to the other side.

Most of the Non-Catholic main line churches have emphasized educational and medical contributions in that other America and have not tried very hard to convert Roman Catholics to become Protestants or “Evangélicos” as they are known there, but they did welcome the interest of those who were curious enough to learn what the Protestants had to offer. One of the areas in which sectarian differences was evident was in Brazil, where the Pentecostals and other groups that stressed evangelization and an emphasis on faith healing, were winning many converts. Their church members built their temples in their free time after their regular work hours. Another means of attraction for some of the people was the use of guitars and other instruments which were played by the members of the congregation and which also increased the volume of the music.

One can notice a dramatic change in the attitude toward the use and importance of the Bible. Whereas, some Protestant groups considered the Bible as pretty much their exclusive property, the approach has changed since Vatican II. In Argentina a group of priests and lay people asked for the help of the Bible Societies in translating the New Testament into the Argentine idiom. Father Alfredo Trusso, then pastor of "Todos Los Santos" (All Saints Church) in Buenos Aires, Padre Jorge Mejía and others asked for cooperation in accomplishing this task. Weeks were spent on Sunday afternoons and evenings to get this task done. Padre Trusso brought a group of his parishioners to visit the Bible House in Buenos Aires and expressed his hope that his church might have something comparable through which to distribute the Bible. This has been quite a turn around over earlier attitudes.

One also saw, particularly in Brazil, the additional influence of voodoo

The Roman Catholic Church may be losing some of its influence in that other America, but in most cases it may be due to the lack of willingness to adapt in any way to the changing forces at work in the world today, the impact of secularism through the media, and other factors which are equally at work in North America.

THE SPIRITS AROUND US

I was a bit surprised by the great number of "espiritistas" in South America, bordering on the world of animism, and they lived in part of the spirit world. They even had their own groups organized for meetings and I remember one continental meeting when they had thousands of people gathered together to have a big meeting of what they called "espiritistas." This was also colored in part by the introduction of voodoo from Africa.

This was more apparent in Brazil than some of the other countries. I remember one night walking along the beach by Copacabana and saw bottles of "Guaraná," which was one of the favorite soft drinks in Brazil. There were candles burning besides the bottles of "Guaraná." I asked about it and my friend said, "This is very important for the spiritists." I said I would like to go over and check out one of those bottles to see how it tasted. He said, "Oh, you can't do that because they are probably watching what we are doing now. Furthermore, they would claim that the flavor of the "Guaraná" would have been removed by the spirits so there would be no use to try to drink it now anyway," and so I didn't even take a sip.

Although I didn't learn either Quechua or Aymará, I did communicate with them fairly well, since they had managed to learn a lot of Spanish. The Indians from the higher Andes spoke Aymará while the Indians around the lower Andes spoke Quechua. Since our main goal was to teach the basics of education as well as English we had no serious conflicts with our Roman Catholic friends and colleagues. Nearly all the Indians as well as "mestizos" were considered and counted by the predominant and official church.

I had met Padres Kirchner and Considine at the American Club in Cochabamba and we exchanged pleasantries. I spoke of the mass baptisms of the Indian children in the mountains and although I secretly thought that many of those children needed a good head washing or shampoo, I agreed that all those colorful ribbons and banners did mark a significant event in the somewhat drab lives of those Indians. My opinion, which amounted to little, suggested that there was a great deal of syncretism, a mixture of animism along with the over all umbrella of Catholicism. Our Maryknoll friends did not seem to be overly concerned and were sure that, in time, they would grow in faith.

The Indian believed in God, it seemed. Jesus Christ to him was a God as was "Sol" (the Sun)) which they called "Inti." It was interesting that in a time of economic crisis the Peruvians changed the name of their basic currency from "Sol" to "Inti." Perhaps they thought that the Indian name would boost confidence in the economy. It didn't seem to help.

Old Saturnino thought that the "Espíritu Santo" (the Holy Spirit) was a kind of "pájaro" (bird). He thought the Holy Virgin was both the mother and wife of "Sol," and he often referred to the "Virgin" in his normal speech. Crispín, however, didn't give much credence to anything. The Indians in Bolivia and in Peru were sure that there were good as well as evil spirits. At crossroads the Indian would pause to place a bit of coca leaves, alcohol or rocks to mollify the spirits. The piles of rocks gave the appearance of shrines. And, of course, land owners knew the fields would produce better crops when cleared of rocks.

As a rule these people seem patient and placid. They seemed to endure great discomforts without complaint, abetted in part possibly by the use of cocaine. The men chewed their coca with a little lime to avoid hunger pangs and seemed to have additional strength and endurance. This was fifty years ago, and I suppose the animistic beliefs have not changed dramatically.

The lack of sanitation as we had known it in the United States was hard for us to accept. That, one might hope, will have changed in the past fifty years. However, we were aware that some of the people seemed to urinate or defecate when and wherever they felt the urge. They would squat along the sidewalk or wherever convenient, especially where two buildings met and there was a comfortable corner to stop. Just off the street and inside the school door seemed to be a favorite spot. These less than sanitary conditions were quite alien to our experience. I don't think that the good spirits of their animistic world gave them any special invisible appearance. They just didn't seem to care. I hope that this custom has been cleaned up by now, but I am sure that the signs of their animistic beliefs are still very much in evidence to this day.

With our revived interest in "angelology" perhaps our guardian angels are also hard at work for us today as well.

LAST RIGHTS AND RITES

It always seems that someone is clamoring for human rights. In that other America less importance is given to the niceties of obsequies or burials. I recall attending the funeral service of a friend in an Andean country. The burial place had not been dug with sufficient care to insure space for the coffin in the underground burial. No special pulleys were used for lowering the casket. Men on each side of the grave held onto the ropes to guide it, but alas, the hole was too narrow or the coffin too wide. After having lowered the box about four or five feet, the box jammed, and it was impossible to get it either up or down. The men began to jiggle and lift it while trying to lower the jammed coffin. They kept up their attempts until with a long handled shovel they were able to widen the grave and were at last able to lower the casket the rest of the way. With all the jerking and jiggling of the box, someone among the mourners came up with an interesting remark. He said, "This is the first time I have seen a body have to do the rhumba on the way down to its final resting place."

Then there was the case of an obese woman. I hadn't realized how big she was until I saw her in the coffin. She had obviously been forced into it. The wooden sides of the coffin had cracked and the glass top for viewing had moved out of place. The wooden coffin gave a creaking or cracking noise even during the funeral service.

An engineer on the Pan American road drowned accidentally in a mountain lake in Bolivia. The law required burial within twenty-four hours. The question was what to do with the body. It was decided to anchor the body until instructions could be received. Cables were sent to relatives in the United States. One reply said to ship the body home, another said to bury him down there. It didn't take the wisdom of Solomon to decide that it was simply easier to have the burial in Bolivia.

HOW DULL COULD IT BE?

I was teaching an evening class. I had noticed that one lady was dozing, but then suddenly she seemed completely out of it. The fact was that she had had a heart attack and died.

I'll never know how much she got out of the class, but my lecture must have been a "killer."

THE TWO AMERICAS

Like the old Indian saying about walking a mile in someone else's shoes, living in another culture for a time helps one to learn about differences and similarities in life experiences. It is easy to become critical about others and their ways. We may tend to think of ours as the very best and that others are well nigh impossible to understand. Nevertheless, if one tries to be objective, it is also possible to understand and appreciate another culture and to see value and excellence in another way of approaching life, its joys and pleasures as well as its adversities and difficulties. It is too simplistic and smug to consider that our ways and our viewpoints are best and uniquely perfect. But rules and our laws may not be as good as we may imagine. It is salutary to hear another voice in the court of public opinion and to learn of things and ideas which may change our perspective while or without losing our own personal pride and appreciation of the values of our own heritage and our own accomplishments.

Although many of my compatriots don't understand it, I can honestly say that the most pleasant years of my life were spent in that other America. I might do some things differently if I had the opportunity to go through those years again, since most of us try to correct and profit from our mistakes.

Environment has had a distinct role to play. The Andes mountains and the tropical areas of that other America have had their influence on its development and progress. There is less of a middle class and the extremes of poverty and wealth are great. Thus far it seems that the opportunities to get ahead are a little more promising in North America. There seems to have been a little more concern for the underprivileged in North America, but the same drives to excel and succeed are present in both.

There is more emphasis on linguistic ability in that other America because generally it means an improved economic situation. People of the North tend to think that everyone should speak in English even though very few of us speak it correctly. The simple rules of grammar may not apply to another language despite our possible belief that ours are superior and ought to be enforced in any and every language. We become so convinced that our own rules and modus operandi are so superior that we try to impose them on others. When will we ever learn that though human nature is basically the same our interpretations often differ. To live together as people of one world, we must some day learn to accept our sameness as well as our difference, since we are all humans trying to live in one world with some what different interpretations of the fundamental rules of society.

Family name and position seemed to mean more in that other America but that situation is rapidly changing. The general attitude is more relaxed and casual, the time pressure is less.

I often said if I were to retire in that other

America, one of the most likely places would have been in the city of Mendoza, Argentina, and I am not "somewhere between San Juan and Mendoza" (an expression meaning inebriated) when I say that.

My health has failed to a degree that keeps me from much travel but I can and do sing "en voz alta," "Viva America del Norte y Viva America del Sur, y que tengan las dos un gran futuro."

> *"Then I came to them of the captivity of Telabib, that dwelt by the river Chebar, and I sat where they sat, and remained there astonished among them seven days."* *Ezekiel 3:15*

ERRATA

Biographical sketch should read: Secretary for Latin America, U.S.A.